15 minute vegan

Katy Beskow

To Tamzin and Tara

15 minute vegan

fast, modern vegan cooking

Katy Beskow

photography by Dan Jones

quadrille

contents

BOBBIN

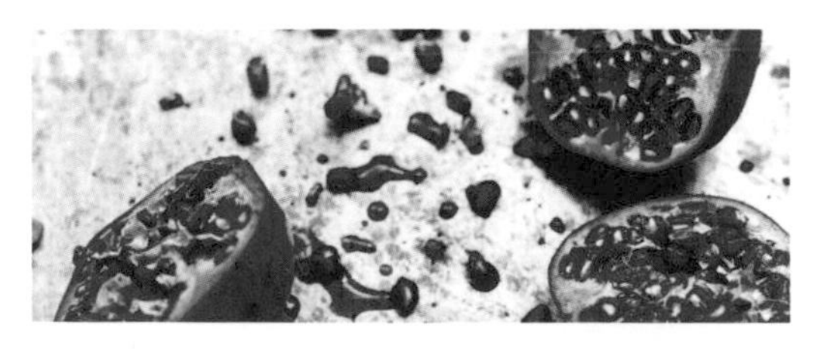

introduction

When I started the vegan recipe blog Little Miss Meat-Free I never dreamed that within a year I would be teaching cooking classes, demonstrating at food festivals, working with a handful of well-known brands and writing for a national magazine. In between these projects, I continued to work full-time at a day job, hustling to ensure the bills were paid so I could carry on with my real passion. As you can imagine, this left me with very little time to cook and enjoy a meal for myself, even though my days were filled with producing elegant dishes, using the best ingredients, for other people to enjoy. I knew that when I got home, I wouldn't want to spend the evening in the kitchen, and that I really didn't have the time (or the inclination) to go shopping for lots of specialist ingredients.

I found that the meals I was cooking at home took fifteen minutes or less to prepare and cook and, as I've never been one to compromise when it comes to flavour, my meals needed to be quick, simple, balanced and delicious. I'd raid the fridge and cupboards, often taking inspiration from the dishes I had cooked earlier that day, but using quicker cooking techniques and ingredients that I had to hand.

The fifteen-minute meals I had created were so delicious I decided to post them on the blog and, to my surprise, these remain my most popular recipes, with lots of readers posting photos of their quick creations across social media. I also challenged friends and family to make my fifteen-minute recipes, rather than ordering takeaways, which led to my title 'Fast Food Queen', as I always had a recipe that was quicker, tastier and a lot cheaper than ordering a takeaway!

I love being in the kitchen and would encourage anyone to develop a passion for good food, however busy their lives. The idyllic dream of wanting to prepare a hearty family meal every evening compared with the reality of the time you actually *have* is often a struggle that is all too real. I believe that great food can be created in even short amounts of time, using fresh ingredients to create something delicious and balanced. I hope you enjoy the time you spend making these recipes as much as you enjoy eating them.

I'm so excited to share my collection of fifteen-minute recipes with you in this book.

Katy Beskow

why vegan?

As a life-long animal lover, I have been a vegetarian from childhood. I became vegan when I moved to London and stumbled across a colourful fruit-and-vegetable market, which left me intoxicated with new sights, fragrances, and tastes. Every Saturday morning, I rushed to the market as early as I could to get the freshest produce and be back in time to be inspired by a day of food TV programmes. I didn't have Nigel Slater's kitchen garden and I couldn't afford to shop in Nigella's delicatessens, but I had a brown paper bag full of colourful fruits and vegetables waiting to be cooked into something delicious (even if it was in the tiniest of kitchens, with just two pans and a cracked jug). I had a limited budget and discovered that by not using any expensive animal ingredients I could experiment even more with flavours and textures.

People choose to become vegan for many reasons, including ethical values, environmental issues, sustainability, reduction of food costs, and health improvement. For me, any health benefit of a vegan diet is a happy side effect of choices that are primarily ethical. More questions are raised about where food is from, the ethics, production, and environmental and humanitarian impact created by what a consumer chooses to purchase and eat. Due to this, there are more people than ever reducing their meat and dairy intake, whether it's to live a vegan lifestyle or simply to try something a bit different in their diet. This book isn't designed as a resource for discussing the politics of veganism, but as a celebration of great, fast food that can be enjoyed by everyone. Vegan food is no longer considered bland and minimalist. If we see past the 'meat-and-two-veg' style of eating and look at better ways to prepare, eat, and enjoy our food, a world of new flavours, textures, and dishes awaits. So many people eat the same old meals, perhaps due to habit or lack of confidence in the kitchen, but not truly enjoying their food, which is a good indication that it is time to shake things up and try new ingredients and methods of cooking.

Reducing dairy and eggs isn't as difficult as it may initially seem. Many of us have a learnt dependence on dairy products, rather than trying something plant-based that can be equally as delicious. Think you can't enjoy a bowl of chilli without a cooling swirl of soured cream? Slice over a creamy avocado. Wonder how you will ever get that soup so thick and rich? Use coconut milk. There's an alternative for everything, which just involves stepping outside the box.

Vegan food lends itself particularly well to fast cooking, as the basic ingredients are easy to prepare and cook. There are fewer food-safety concerns compared with the storage, preparation, and use of meat, fish, dairy, and eggs; just be sure to wash your fresh vegetables thoroughly, store non-dairy milk and yoghurt products in the refrigerator, and ensure any beans and pulses are cooked thoroughly before consuming. Great vegan food doesn't have to be complicated – and I promise it won't be bland. Every recipe in this book has been tested to ensure it is packed with flavour, using the simplest and fastest methods. After all, we want to be eating the food, not waiting for it to cook!

how to cook in 15 minutes

Being short of time doesn't mean you have to sacrifice cooking great food or be a culinary genius to achieve it. With a few simple tips, time-saving advice, and tried-and-tested recipes, you'll be eating the best food in no time. Many people think that fast cooking must involve preparing all your ingredients ahead of time, but this is not the case. Simply using your time effectively before and during the process is all that is needed.

1. If you're using the oven, set it to preheat as soon as you decide what to cook.

2. If you need to add hot water or stock to a recipe, get the kettle on before you start, so you have less time to wait once you start the cooking process.

3. When a recipe calls for the use of a pan or wok, add the oil in and get it over the recommended heat level before you do anything else. You can then prepare the first vegetable required with no time waiting for the pan to reach temperature.

4. There's no need to prepare all the ingredients before you start cooking. Start with the items that have the longest cooking time, then while these are cooking, you can prepare and then add the other ingredients. Don't worry if you're unsure of what should come first – I've listed the preparation step-by-step in each recipe's method.

5. If you have more time and plan on fast cooking later, you can prepare many ingredients in advance, if you wish. Keep prepared fruits and vegetables refrigerated and in sealed glass jars, then bring to room temperature before cooking.

6. Have a selection of useful kitchen equipment to reach: a couple of good-quality knives, a wooden spoon, garlic press, measuring spoons, and a timer.

7. Fresh ingredients such as vegetables and fruits are often easier to peel, chop, and work with when they are at room temperature. Produce which is in season is more tender and tastes better, so work with what is commonly available.

8. Have a storecupboard (pantry) stocked with essentials such as pasta, rice, flour, and sugar; that way you have all the basics to hand for when you want to cook something (with no running to the shop!). I keep dried items in tall jars, so they are easy to find in the cupboard without having to search for half-used packets.

9. Taste your food as you cook, adding more seasoning to suit your taste. Don't be a slave to a recipe – if the addition of more or less of an ingredient works for you, then go with it. Trust your instincts.

10. Get some music on, pour yourself a glass of wine, or brew a cup of tea and enjoy cooking! Too many people find cooking a chore; relax, get creative, and reap the benefits.

storecupboard essentials

Having a storecupboard (pantry) stocked with a few essentials means that you're always prepared to cook up something delicious in no time at all. Forget about pre-prepared meals, as they can be expensive and lacking in flavour. Instead, have some basic ingredients to hand so you can create a home-cooked dish whenever you want.

beans and pulses

Beans and pulses are versatile staples of a vegan diet, offering substance and a healthy source of protein and fibre to any dish. However, they are renowned for taking hours to prepare before you can start cooking with them. Instead, canned beans and pulses only require draining and rinsing before you can use them. Always rinse well through a sieve to remove the salted water solution and to remove that 'canned' taste. Keep a selection of canned beans and pulses in your cupboard, including red kidney beans, butter (lima) beans, green lentils, and chickpeas.

nuts and seeds

These are the ultimate fast ingredients, instantly ready to add texture and crunch to any dish – think of a sweet pecan topping over pancakes or a sprinkle of sesame seeds over Pad Thai jay (see page 106). Store in airtight jars to keep them at their optimum flavour and freshness. Nuts and seeds are also nutritional powerhouses, full of essential fatty acids, protein, and fibre. Try a few varieties and discover what works well with other flavours, keeping a few basics in your cupboard, including walnuts, flaked (slivered) almonds, sesame seeds, and pistachios.

yeast extract

Love it or hate it, yeast extract is a magical ingredient when you are short of time. A teaspoon of the dark elixir stirred through a sauce will give it a deeper, richer flavour, as though it's been cooked for hours. If you'd vowed never to eat it on toast, don't dismiss it is a fantastic basic ingredient in fast cooking. Still need some encouragement? Try it in my One-pot chilli (see page 92).

herbs, spices, and blends

Invest in a few jars of herbs and spices, so you always have the basics to create a full-of-flavour dish, no matter how much time you can spare in the kitchen. Woody herbs such as rosemary, thyme, sage, and oregano are preserved beautifully as dried herbs and enrich the base flavour of a dish. Leafier herbs such as parsley, coriander (cilantro), basil, and mint are best kept on your windowsill and used fresh. Have a selection of your favourite sweet and savoury spices in your cupboard, including cinnamon, ground ginger, cumin, and turmeric. Spice and herb blends require no pre-toasting – think mixed chilli powder, herbes de Provence, and garam masala. There is often snobbery around using a concentrated curry paste – it may not be fully authentic to the dish you are making, but it is a fantastic way to pack a flavour punch with a blend of spices, particularly when you are short of time.

pasta

This is the ultimate fast food and a staple in any household cupboard. It's available in many shapes, sizes, wheats, and colours, making it the perfect base ingredient for a number of dishes. Most dried pasta sold in the supermarkets is egg free, but double-check to be sure. Pasta is a low-cost ingredient, which will keep well in your cupboard stored in its sealed bag or in a clip jar. Have a selection of penne, spaghetti, tagliatelle, and macaroni as standard.

antipasti vegetables

Vegetables preserved in oil are a useful ingredient for any cook, particularly when you want to create a great dish with little time. The vegetables are roasted, charred, or sundried before being submerged in the oil, ready to use, cutting out that lengthy cooking time. Have a selection of jarred antipasti vegetables, including artichokes, sundried tomatoes, peppers, and mixed mushrooms – perfect for when you need maximum flavour.

ketchup and sauces

Never think of ketchup just as a dipping sauce. Squeeze a tablespoon of ketchup into tomato-based dishes and sauces for instant seasoning. Have your favourite sauces, including barbecue, sweet chilli, and mustard available to add extra quick flavour! Always read the labels on shop-bought labels as they can contain hidden non-vegan ingredients.

rice

This makes a wonderful side dish or pudding, and is extremely versatile as a staple for your storecupboard. Opt for basmati, jasmine, American long grain, and flaked rice for the fastest cooking times, and save wild and brown rice for when you have more time in the kitchen.

oils

The purpose of oil when cooking is to bring the pan to a high temperature so that heat can be transferred to the food, thus promoting fast and effective cooking. It can also be used to add flavour to finished dishes, as well as adding moisture to baked goods. I'd recommend using a mild-flavoured oil (such as sunflower or olive oil) for general cooking and baking, and a good-quality pressed oil (such as extra virgin olive or rapeseed oil) for drizzling over finished products. Coconut oil is best used in puddings because its sweeter flavour can overpower a savoury dish.

a note on sugar

Sugar provides natural sweetness and should be enjoyed in moderation. Although I disagree with 'hidden sugars' in food, I use sugar where required in home baking, including caster (superfine), granulated, demerara, golden syrup, and maple syrup (but not all at once!). Most of the sugar sold in the UK is not combined with, or filtered through, animal products, making it suitable for vegans. If you are unsure, contact the supplier or research online.

a note on salt

A sprinkling of salt enhances both sweet and savoury flavours, lifting a dish from everyday to exceptional. Use good-quality salt flakes and gently crush them between your fingers as you scatter moderately over your food.

fast, fresh essentials

Fast cooking calls for fresh ingredients that are easy to prepare and cook down quickly. It's always worth having a selection of fresh ingredients in your refrigerator, so when the need for a fast meal arises, you have the essentials to hand.

Soft fruits, such as blueberries, raspberries, strawberries, grapes, and blackberries, require no preparation and can be used for a quick morning smoothie, simple snack, or baked into a crumble for pudding. Other low-preparation fruits include peaches, nectarines, bananas, and cherries. Choose your fruits seasonally for the best flavour, price, and variety all year round. It's worth keeping a couple of peeled, ripe bananas in the freezer to throw into smoothies or whip up a Banana split ice cream (see page 115).

Lemons and limes provide fast bursts of flavour in a dish when the juice is squeezed over at the end of cooking. Always choose unwaxed fruits as they are often waxed for aesthetic purposes with an animal ingredient such as shellac, which is not suitable for vegans. Squeeze lemons and limes when they are at room temperature to get the most juice out of them.

Most vegetables can be quick-cooked, depending on the method you use. Some vegetables, including mushrooms, tomatoes, peppers, and long-stem broccoli, cook quickly, while other root vegetables require longer cooking times. Look out for vacuum-packed, pre-cooked root vegetables, like beetroot, which normally require a long roasting time, but whose pre-cooked versions can be simply sliced before eating. Opt for versatile vegetables, such as spinach, which can be served as a salad leaf or added into a curry; kale, which can be stir-fried or crisp-roasted; and celery, which can be used as a base flavour for cooked dishes or to give added crunch to salads. Sweetcorn, peas, edamame beans, and butternut squash all retain their great taste and texture when frozen, making for a convenient and economical way to enjoy these vegetables.

Onions and garlic make for a fast, flavoursome base to many dishes when used either together or individually. Have a selection of brown and red onions to hand for variety, and keep them in a cool, dark place for longevity.

Fresh herbs, such as parsley, coriander (cilantro), and mint can be quickly torn or chopped and added to a dish to take it from simple to superb, adding layers of fresh flavour. If you have the space, grow them in a window box or keep them refrigerated, stem-down in a jar of water. Basil is best stored at room temperature.

If you're new to dairy-free cooking, try the many ranges of milk available, including soya, almond, cashew, macadamia, oat, and rice. Many are available as sweetened or non-sweetened, so choose which suits you best. I tend to opt for an unsweetened soya milk for use in cooking, alongside a nut milk for drinks and desserts. A pot of non-dairy yoghurt is also a useful ingredient to keep in your refrigerator; for use in a savoury dish, opt for an unsweetened, sugar-free soya yoghurt. Sweetened or flavoured soya yoghurt is best used in sweet dishes.

If you enjoy cheese, do try the ever-growing range of vegan cheeses now available in most supermarkets and health-food shops.

When a recipe in this book calls for coconut milk, it refers to the full-fat canned variety, which is thick and creamy, not to be confused with the blended coconut milks which you'll find chilled in cartons.

I make no apologies for using shop-bought pastry; it's quick, fuss-free, and even top-name chefs like the convenience of a pre-made pastry sheet. I tend to keep a supply of shortcrust, puff, and filo, ready for a speedy supper or dessert. Store in the freezer or refrigerator and allow to come to room temperature before using for best results. Many brands are accidentally vegan, using vegetable fats instead of butter – simply check in the ingredients list before you buy.

Wine and beer can be added to a dish to give a hearty, warming flavour or enjoyed alongside your meal, although some varieties contain eggs, gelatine, and isinglass, which is derived from the swim bladders of fish. Check with your supplier or do some research on one of the many great online resources. Do bear in mind that brands change their ingredients from time to time, so be sure to check before re-purchasing.

useful kitchen equipment

A few good-quality knives will make chopping much quicker. For home cooking, I'd recommend a small, medium, large, and a bread knife. Look for knives that are weighty yet ergonomic and buy the best you can afford – they will last you a lifetime if you look after them well. Alongside knives, a non-slip chopping board makes preparing ingredients hassle-free. Wooden boards offer protection for your knife blades, as they absorb the impact of the knife better than plastic or glass boards.

When cooking in 15 minutes, opt for pans that are silver or black inside as they heat up quickly. Often, casserole dishes have a white lining internally; these are best kept for slow-cooking. Woks are also great at fast cooking due to their concave shape.

A high-powered blender is a great investment piece and can be used to whip up the creamiest sauce, smoothest pesto, and even make ice cream! Blenders with a power of over 1000W have the best capabilities and versatility.

Measuring spoons give accurate amounts of tablespoons and teaspoons, which are more precise than the measures from the cutlery in your drawer. Food processors slice, chop, and shred vegetables, mix ingredients and can even knead dough. They differ from blenders as the interchangeable blades work better with drier ingredients, allowing you full control of how you want an ingredient prepared.

A garlic press is a cheap, easy-to-find gadget that saves lots of time in the kitchen. Simply place the clove into the device and squeeze the handle to crush the garlic. The skin will come away smoothly.

breakfast

cinnamon toast
vanilla yoghurt and warm berry compote
tomato-stuffed field mushrooms
spiced apple oat pots
passion fruit and lavender porridge
grilled banana and chocolate sandwiches
sticky nutmeg and date palmiers
grilled grapefruit with maple syrup and pecans
edamame beans on toast with lemon and chives
courgette and thyme scones
zesty orange and lemon waffles
breakfast burritos
watermelon, cucumber, and mint breakfast salad
smashed avocado, parsley, and tomato bagels
cranberry and orange granola
almond butter morning cookies
carrot and ginger zinger
peanut butter and banana milkshake
cherry and garden mint smoothie bowl
fastest fruit smoothie

cinnamon toast

serves 4

Lazy mornings are made for sticky, messy breakfasts and sugary lips. Treat yourself to this sweet, French-style toast, with a coffee, perhaps over the morning newspapers.

Get the oil nice and hot in a griddle pan as you make the batter so it will be ready to cook your cinnamon toast as soon as you are.

4 tablespoons sunflower oil

200ml (7fl oz/scant 1 cup) soya milk

2 tablespoons maple syrup

2 teaspoons vanilla extract

100g plain (3½oz/¾ cup) plain (all-purpose) flour

1¼ teaspoons ground cinnamon

4 slices of thick white bread

2 tablespoons granulated sugar

Start by heating the oil in a griddle pan over a medium to high heat while you make the batter.

In a bowl, whisk together the soya milk, maple syrup and vanilla extract. Then stir in the flour and 1 teaspoon of cinnamon. Mix together until it forms a smooth paste.

Dip a slice of bread into the batter and coat both sides. Use tongs to place the slice of bread onto the griddle pan, turning after 2 minutes when it is golden and crisp. Repeat with each slice of bread, keeping the others warm on top of each other on a plate lined with kitchen paper (paper towel).

Mix the sugar and remaining cinnamon in a small bowl and sprinkle over each slice before serving.

vanilla yoghurt with warm berry compote

serves 2

There is something decadent about ice-cold yoghurt topped with warm, sticky berries; it tastes more like a dessert than a breakfast, which is never a bad thing. Unexpectedly, the sweetness comes from the vanilla yoghurt, while the warm berry compote has a lemon hit. These soft berries break down easily during cooking and make the fastest compote, but do experiment with other berries as the seasons change.

Add the blackberries, raspberries, and blueberries to a saucepan. Use a fork to crush them slightly, then cook over a medium heat for 5 minutes, stirring frequently.

Add the lemon juice to the pan, then cook down for a further 2 minutes.

Spoon the yoghurt into glasses or bowls, then pour over the compote. Decorate with mint leaves and serve warm.

100g (3½oz/¾ cup) blackberries

100g (3½oz/scant 1 cup) raspberries

100g (3½oz/¾ cup) blueberries

juice of 1 unwaxed lemon

500g (1lb 2oz/2 cups) non-dairy vanilla yoghurt

fresh mint leaves, to decorate

tomato-stuffed field mushrooms

serves 2

I love these herby mushrooms served over thick slices of toast for brunch. They also make the perfect addition to any pasta dish later in the day.

Preheat the oven as you prepare the mushrooms to ensure optimum cooking quality.

Preheat the oven to 200°C/400°F/Gas 6.

Remove the stems of the mushrooms and discard. Arrange the mushrooms on a baking tray, flat-side up, and fill with the cherry tomatoes.

Drizzle with the oil and sprinkle with the thyme and oregano. Bake for 13–14 minutes until tender.

Season with sea salt just before serving.

4 large field mushrooms

12–16 cherry tomatoes

2 tablespoons olive oil

pinch of dried thyme

pinch of dried oregano

pinch of sea salt

spiced apple oat pots

serves 2

These comforting pots of apple, oats, and cinnamon are comforting and warming. This is one that all the family will love.

Add the oats, almond milk, cinnamon, and ginger to a pan and cook over a medium heat for 3 minutes.

When the oats appear creamy, stir through the apple and raisins, then cook for a further 2–3 minutes. Serve immediately.

100g (3½oz/1 cup) rolled oats

250ml (9fl oz/1 cup) almond milk

½ teaspoon ground cinnamon

½ teaspoon ground ginger

1 red apple, grated

1 tablespoon jumbo raisins

passion fruit and lavender porridge

serves 2

Enjoy that homely scent of porridge bubbling in a pan. Add the subtle flavour of lavender and top with exotic, fruity passion fruit for a naturally sweet breakfast. Be sure to choose lavender extract without artificial flavours, for the best taste.

Add the oats and soya milk to a pan and gently bring to the boil for 4–5 minutes over a low-medium heat. Spoon through the lavender extract, increase the heat to medium, and cook for another 2 minutes, stirring frequently.

Whilst the porridge is cooking, cut the passion fruits in half. Spoon the porridge into bowls and scoop out the seedy flesh of the passion fruits, serving over the porridge.

100g (3½oz/1 cup) rolled oats

300ml (10fl oz/1¼ cups) sweetened soya milk

½ teaspoon lavender extract

2 passion fruits

grilled banana and chocolate sandwiches

serves 2

Once tried,
never forgotten.
You're welcome.

4 slices of thick white bread

vegan margarine, for spreading

2 ripe bananas

2 tablespoons dark chocolate chips

Heat a dry griddle pan over a high heat while you prepare the sandwiches.

Spread only one side of the bread with margarine.

In a small bowl, mash the bananas and stir in the chocolate chips.

Spoon the mixture onto the side of the bread with no margarine. Sandwich with the other slice of bread, so the margarine side is facing upwards. This will stop the sandwich sticking to the pan. Repeat for the other sandwich.

Using a spatula, lift the sandwiches onto the hot griddle pan. Cook for 2–3 minutes until crisp before flipping over and cooking the other side.

Slice in half and serve immediately.

sticky nutmeg and date palmiers

serves 4

French-style patisserie will forever be known for being delicious, beautiful, and crafted by masters. These palmiers (or pig's ears as they are often called) are so easy to make with a simple roll-in technique. Most major brands of prepared puff pastry are made with oil instead of butter, but always check the ingredients before purchasing. Choose a variety that is pre-rolled to save time.

Keep the puff pastry chilled until just before you use it so it doesn't become sticky or difficult to work with.

1 sheet of shop-bought puff pastry (ensure dairy free)

1 tablespoon caster (superfine) sugar

½ teaspoon grated nutmeg

4 stoned (pitted) dates

1 tablespoon soya milk, to glaze

Preheat the oven to 220°C/425°F/Gas 7.

Flatten the pastry sheet on a large board and scatter with the sugar. Grate over the nutmeg and smooth onto the pastry.

Chop the dates into small pieces and scatter over the pastry.

Fold each long side over to meet in the centre, then fold over once more to meet in the centre again.

Using a sharp knife, cut diagonal slices, approximately 2cm (¾in) thick. Arrange cut-side down onto a baking tray, allowing for some spreading.

Brush over the soya milk and bake for 10 minutes until golden brown.

grilled grapefruit with maple syrup and pecans

serves 2

Pink grapefruits are juicy, sweet, and refreshing - perfect for breakfast with maple syrup and crunchy pecan nuts.

It's easier and quicker to peel grapefruits when they are at room temperature.

Heat a griddle pan over a medium-high heat while you prepare the grapefruits.

Peel the grapefruits and cut them into 1cm (½in) slices. Remove any visible seeds.

Pour the maple syrup and cinnamon into a bowl and mix together. Dip each grapefruit slice in the syrup, then use tongs to place on the griddle pan.

Cook for 30 seconds, then turn to cook the other side.

Transfer onto plates and drizzle with the extra maple syrup. Scatter over the pecans and enjoy hot.

2 pink grapefruits

4 tablespoons maple syrup, plus an extra 4 tablespoons for drizzling

½ teaspoon ground cinnamon

handful of crushed pecans

edamame beans on toast with lemon and chives

serves 2

Garlic, lemon, and chives season edamame beans beautifully in this modern twist on a breakfast classic.

Frozen edamame beans are available from many large supermarkets. They are very versatile, so keep a handy bag in the freezer.

1 tablespoon olive oil

6 tablespoons edamame (soya) beans

1 clove of garlic, crushed

juice of 1 unwaxed lemon

small handful of chives, finely chopped

pinch of coarse sea salt

2 thick slices of sourdough

drizzle of extra virgin olive oil (optional)

4 cherry tomatoes, quartered

In a pan, heat the olive oil and edamame beans over a high heat for 2 minutes. Add the garlic to the pan and quickly stir-fry for another minute.

Reduce the heat to low-medium. Add the lemon juice to the pan. Stir the chives through the beans along with the salt. Cook for a further minute and then smash the beans roughly.

Lightly toast the bread until crisp and golden. Pile the beans high on the bread and drizzle with extra virgin olive oil for an added fruity flavour, if desired. Top with tomatoes before serving.

courgette and thyme scones

makes about 6 medium scones

Warm, herby scones are perfect any time of the day, especially for breakfast and brunch. Serve with lashings of vegan cream cheese.

No time to grate the courgette? Just add it to a food processor until shredded.

500g (1lb 2oz/4 cups) plain (all-purpose) flour, plus extra for dusting

½ teaspoon bicarbonate of soda (baking soda)

1 rounded teaspoon dried thyme, finely chopped

1 teaspoon dried mixed herbs

1 medium courgette (zucchini)

pinch of salt and freshly ground black pepper

300ml (10fl oz/1¼ cups) unsweetened soya milk, plus an extra 2 teaspoons for glazing

Preheat the oven to 220°C/425°F/Gas 7.

In a bowl, mix together the flour, bicarbonate of soda, thyme, and mixed herbs.

Grate the courgette and squeeze out the excess moisture. Add it to the bowl and stir through, ensuring it is coated in the flour mixture to avoid the courgette sinking to the bottom of the scones. Season with salt and pepper.

Pour in the soya milk and mix to combine into a dough.

Roll the dough out onto a lightly floured surface to about 3cm (1¼in) thick. Using a scone cutter, cut out the scones and place them onto a baking tray.

Use a pastry brush to glaze the top with the soya milk.

Bake for 12 minutes until the tops are just golden.

zesty orange and lemon waffles

serves 2

I'm often told that many of my recipes have an American influence. When I started out as vegan in 2006, many of my resources and recipes were from the US. I loved so many of the ingredients and I still use them over ten years later. These hot orange and lemon breakfast waffles hold a special place in my heart – is there any wonder why I love so many American breakfasts?

The batter will keep overnight in the refrigerator, so you can make it in advance for an even faster waffle fix in the morning.

250g (9oz/2 cups) self-raising (self-rising) flour

1 teaspoon baking powder

1 tablespoon granulated sugar

300ml (10fl oz/1¼ cups) soya milk

70ml (3fl oz/⅓ cup) orange juice

70ml (3fl oz/⅓ cup) sunflower oil

1 teaspoon vanilla extract

zest and juice of 1 unwaxed lemon

Heat your waffle maker according to its instructions.

In a large bowl, mix together the flour, baking powder and sugar.

Pour in the soya milk, orange juice, oil, and vanilla extract and mix until just combined.

Pour the batter into the waffle maker and cook for 8–10 minutes. While the waffles are cooking, grate the zest of the lemon and squeeze out the juice, reserving for when the waffles are cooked.

Carefully remove the waffles from the machine. Drizzle with the lemon juice and scatter over the lemon zest. Serve immediately.

breakfast burritos

serves 2

Burritos make the best on-the-go breakfasts. Simply wrap them up in some kitchen foil to keep them hot!

In a large frying pan or wok, heat the oil over a high heat.

Add the red pepper and spring onions to the pan and cook for 1–2 minutes.

Add the cannellini beans to the pan along with the chilli powder, smoked paprika, and cumin. Stir frequently, crushing the beans slightly, cooking for a further 2 minutes.

Remove the pan from the heat and stir through the lime juice, coriander, and red chilli.

Lay out the wraps and load in the hot filling. Scatter mix with coriander and avocado slices to garnish. Fold in until secure.

1 tablespoon sunflower oil

1 red (bell) pepper, sliced into strips

2 spring onions (scallions), roughly chopped

235g (8oz) can cannellini beans, rinsed and drained

1 teaspoon mild chilli powder

1 teaspoon smoked paprika

½ teaspoon ground cumin

juice of 1 unwaxed lime

handful of fresh coriander (cilantro), plus extra to garnish

1 red chilli, deseeded and finely sliced

1 large avocado, finely sliced

4 soft tortilla wraps

watermelon, cucumber, and mint breakfast salad

serves 2

Light and refreshing, this dish is perfect alone or as an addition to a heartier breakfast.

Slice the watermelon into chunky strips and remove the skin.

Chop the cucumber into thin pieces, leaving the skin on for extra texture. Combine in a bowl with the grapes.

Add the mint to the bowl. Squeeze over the lime juice and serve immediately.

¼ large watermelon

½ cucumber

handful of green grapes

4 fresh mint leaves, finely chopped

juice of ½ unwaxed lime

smashed avocado, parsley, and tomato bagels

serves 2

If you love avocado on toast, these bagels offer a flavoursome twist. Cool, smashed avocado meets zingy lime, fresh parsley, and sweet tomatoes, loaded onto a hot, crisp-soft bagel.

2 savoury bagels

2 ripe avocados

handful of fresh flat-leaf parsley, roughly chopped

3 cherry tomatoes, roughly chopped

juice of 1 unwaxed lime

generous pinch of sea salt

Slice the bagels in half and toast until golden.

In the meantime, make the topping. Remove the stones from the avocados and scoop the flesh into a bowl. Mash with a fork until some parts are smooth and some bits are still chunky. Stir the parsley and tomatoes into the avocado. Stir in the lime juice and sprinkle with sea salt.

Spoon the topping over the hot bagels and serve immediately.

cranberry and orange granola

serves 2

This chewy granola tastes like it's been slow baked, although it's actually made in less than five minutes. Gently toasting the almonds and oats in a hot pan brings out all those slow-cooked flavours, while the maple syrup adds a smoky background taste. You'll never make granola the same way again.

Get the hot granola straight into the refrigerator for 10 minutes to set if you want to eat it straight away. If you are blessed with more time, lay it out onto a baking sheet and allow it to cool to room temperature overnight.

Toast the almonds and oats in a dry pan over a medium heat for 2 minutes, stirring frequently.

Spoon in the coconut oil, maple syrup, and dried cranberries and stir through to ensure all the oats are coated. Cook through for 2 minutes, stirring continuously, then grate over the orange zest.

Spoon the granola evenly onto a baking tray, allowing natural clumps of oats to form as they settle. Place the tray in the refrigerator for 10 minutes before serving.

Serve in a bowl with fresh fruit and soya yoghurt.

1 tablespoon blanched almonds

100g (3½oz/1 cup) rolled oats

1 tablespoon coconut oil, at room temperature

2 tablespoons maple syrup

1 tablespoon dried cranberries

zest of 1 unwaxed orange

almond butter morning cookies

makes 4 cookies

When the need for a breakfast cookie arises, these chewy little delights will come to the rescue. They are balanced enough to eat for breakfast, yet chocolatey enough to save for your 11am coffee. These cookies are packed with energy-giving nuts, oats, and, ahem, chocolate chips. Almond butter is readily available from health-food shops and large supermarkets, and is a welcome ingredient to any storecupboard (pantry).

3 tablespoons almond butter

2 tablespoons rolled oats

2 tablespoons almond milk

1 tablespoon dark chocolate chips

1½ tablespoon flaked (slivered) almonds

Preheat the oven to 200°C/400°F/Gas 6.

In a bowl, spoon in the almond butter, rolled oats, and almond milk and mix until combined.

Stir in the chocolate chips and 1 tablespoon flaked almonds until a stiff dough forms.

Use your hands to roll out the dough into balls, then flatten onto a baking sheet.

Bake for 12 minutes, or until just golden. In the meantime, toast the remaining flaked almonds in a dry pan until they have just turned golden. Best eaten warm with a sprinkle of toasted almonds.

carrot and ginger zinger

serves 2

A freshly pressed juice is the perfect accompaniment to any breakfast. I love this one because it uses up what's left at the back of the refrigerator – waste not, want not!

The most time-consuming part of making a fresh juice is cleaning the juicer afterwards. So, make double the quantity, pour into an airtight jar and store in the refrigerator for up to three days.

Run the carrots, apples, and ginger through a juicer.

Serve in glasses over ice.

4 carrots, washed and chilled

2 red apples (stems and pips removed if your home juicer requires)

2cm (¾in) piece of ginger, peeled

4 ice cubes

peanut butter and banana milkshake

serves 2

Start the day with a classic flavour combination – perfect.

Keep peanut butter stored at room temperature for the easiest and fastest way to spoon from the jar.

Spoon the peanut butter into a blender and break in the bananas. Add in the strawberries along with the almond milk. Blend on high until completely smooth.

2 tablespoons of smooth peanut butter

2 ripe bananas

4 strawberries

400ml (14fl oz/1¾ cups) almond milk

cherry and garden mint smoothie bowl

serves 2

Is there a prettier way to start your day than with this fresh and fruity smoothie bowl? This smoothie is so thick that you can eat it with a spoon and place toppings over it for added flavour, crunch, and substance.

Add the frozen cherries, banana, soya yoghurt, mint, and almond milk to a blender and blend on high until completely smooth.

Pour into bowls and top with the flaked almonds and sour cherries.

200g (7oz/1¼ cups) frozen cherries

1 banana, roughly chopped

1 tablespoon sweetened soya yoghurt

handful of fresh mint leaves

100ml (3½oz/scant ½ cup) almond milk

2 tablespoons flaked (slivered) almonds

1 tablespoon dried sour cherries

fastest fruit smoothie

serves 2

If you avoid smoothies because you don't have time to chop and prepare a lots of fruits, then this is your new go-to smoothie!

Use a high-powered blender for the fastest smoothies. A good blender is an investment piece and an invaluable time-saving tool.

Add all the ingredients into a blender and blitz on high until completely smooth.

½ punnet of strawberries, stalks removed but green leaves remaining

½ punnet of blueberries

½ punnet of raspberries

½ punnet of blackberries

handful of baby spinach leaves

300ml (10fl oz/1¼ cups) almond milk, chilled

light bites

red coconut bisque
sweetcorn chowder
smoky chickpea soup
red pepper gazpacho
courgette, pea, and watercress minestrone
rustic ribollita
crispy potato rosti
sweet tomato bruschetta with olive tapenade
pitta pizzas
satay noodles
carrot and cardamom falafel
pea and garden mint fritters
orange, pomegranate, and pistachio pilaf
sweet jacket potatoes with yoghurt, pomegranate, and toasted walnuts
tempura vegetables with a soy, chilli, and coriander dipping sauce
edamame, lime, and sesame jar salad
caramelized fig and pistachio salad
beetroot and pickled walnut salad with minted yoghurt
squash and orange salad with hazelnuts
grilled baby gem, asparagus, and petits pois salad

red coconut bisque

serves 4

This indulgent bisque is silky and creamy with a subtle eastern flavour. It's a seriously addictive bowl of indulgence.

Shop-bought Thai red curry paste is a time-saver as the spices are pre-mixed – just ensure it does not contain fish sauce. Keep this handy little jar in the refrigerator for up to four weeks.

2 teaspoons olive oil

1 onion, finely chopped

2 cloves of garlic, crushed

2cm (¾in) piece of ginger, peeled and finely chopped

2 tablespoons Thai red curry paste

400ml (14fl oz) can full-fat coconut milk

800ml (28fl oz/3½ cups) hot vegetable stock

2 carrots, grated

6 tomatoes, roughly chopped

handful of coconut flakes

1 unwaxed lime

handful of fresh coriander (cilantro), roughly chopped

2 spring onions (scallions), sliced on the diagonal

In a large pan, heat the oil over a low-medium heat. Add the onion to the pan and cook for 2 minutes. Add the garlic and ginger and cook for a further minute, along with the Thai red curry paste.

Pour in the coconut milk and vegetable stock and increase the heat to medium-high. Bring to the boil. Add the carrots and tomatoes to the pan and cook for 8 minutes, stirring occasionally.

Add the coconut flakes to a dry pan and toast over a medium heat for 2 minutes, set aside.

Remove the bisque pan from the heat and transfer to a blender, or use a hand-held blender and blitz until completely smooth. Squeeze in the lime juice through a sieve and pour into bowls. Scatter with the coriander, spring onions, and coconut flakes just before serving.

sweetcorn chowder

serves 4

I love the smoky background to this classic soup, which is sunny in both colour and flavour. Using frozen sweetcorn reduces the cooking time and it's likely you'll always have some in the freezer ready to make this hearty soup.

Smoked paprika deepens the flavour of this chowder and makes it taste as though it has been cooking for hours, not for less than 15 minutes!

In a large pan, heat the oil over a medium heat. Add the onion, then throw the red pepper, celery, and chilli flakes into the pan and cook for 2–3 minutes until softened.

Tip in the sweetcorn, vegetable stock, and coconut milk and increase the heat to high. Stir through the smoked paprika, then partially cover with a lid. Cook for 10 minutes, stirring occasionally.

Remove from the heat and season with sea salt. Ladle half the soup into a blender and blast until completely smooth. Pour the smooth half back into the unblended soup and combine. Serve hot with spring onions, coriander and a wedge of lime to garnish.

1 tablespoon sunflower oil

1 onion, roughly chopped

1 red (bell) pepper, finely sliced

1 celery stick, chopped

¼ teaspoon chilli flakes

300g (10oz/1¼ cups) frozen sweetcorn

800ml (28fl oz/3½ cups) hot vegetable stock

400ml (14fl oz) can full-fat coconut milk

1 rounded teaspoon smoked paprika

pinch of sea salt

2 spring onions (scallions), sliced on the diagonal

handful of fresh coriander (cilantro)

1 lime, quartered

smoky chickpea soup

serves 4

Prepare for layers of flavour from this Moroccan-inspired soup. The first spoonful tastes of salted lemons and sweet cinnamon, the next fragrant cumin and turmeric with the added depth of smoked paprika and harissa. Serve with warm flatbreads.

This soup can be frozen for up to four weeks for a simple light meal when you don't have 15 minutes to spare!

Heat the oil in a large pan over a low-medium heat, then add the onion to the pan. Throw in the garlic and celery. Cook for 2 minutes until the onion has softened but not browned.

Spoon in the cumin, harissa, turmeric, cinnamon, and paprika and coat the onion, garlic, and celery. Tip in the tomatoes and vegetable stock, increasing the heat to medium-high.

Add the chickpeas to the pan along with the kale. Cover with a lid and cook for 10 minutes, stirring frequently.

Remove the soup from the heat after 10 minutes and squeeze in the lemon juice through a sieve and scatter with the parsley. Season with sea salt.

1 tablespoon olive oil

1 onion, finely chopped

1 clove of garlic, crushed

2 celery sticks, finely chopped

2 teaspoons ground cumin

1 teaspoon harissa paste

½ teaspoon ground turmeric

½ teaspoon ground cinnamon

½ teaspoon smoked paprika

400g (14oz) can chopped tomatoes

600ml (20fl oz/2½ cups) hot vegetable stock

240g (8½oz) can chickpeas (garbanzo beans), rinsed and drained

2 handfuls of kale

1 unwaxed lemon

1 handful of fresh flat-leaf parsley, roughly chopped

generous sprinkle of sea salt

red pepper gazpacho

serves 2

For those days when you don't want to turn on the oven, this full-of-flavour gazpacho is the perfect light bite. If you keep the vegetables chilled until you are ready to use them, then this gazpacho will require no refrigeration.

This gazpacho will keep in the refrigerator for up to three days when stored in a sealed jar or container.

Roughly slice the red peppers and discard the tops and seeds and add to a blender with the cucumber and spring onions.

Throw in the tomatoes and tomato juice, along with the coriander. Blend on high until almost smooth.

Season with sea salt before serving.

2 red (bell) peppers

½ cucumber, roughly chopped

3 spring onions (scallions), roughly chopped

6 plum tomatoes

200ml (7fl oz/scant 1 cup) tomato juice, chilled

generous handful of fresh coriander (cilantro)

pinch of sea salt

courgette, pea, and watercress minestrone

serves 4

This is a traditional soup with a seasonal twist. Spring pea and courgette offer a fresher flavour to this soup. Although it's a light meal it will satisfy all the family. I use small strands of broken spaghetti in this dish as it's something I always have in my storecupboard (pantry), but feel free to experiment with other small pasta varieties. Keep this soup chunky and serve it with wedges of crusty bread.

1 tablespoon sunflower oil

1 onion, roughly chopped

100g (3½oz) asparagus tips

1 medium courgette (zucchini), chopped

2 celery sticks, chopped

300ml (10fl oz/1¼ cups) hot vegetable stock

400g (14oz) can chopped tomatoes

2 teaspoons dried mixed herbs

30g (1oz) dried spaghetti

2 handfuls of watercress

3 tablespoons frozen peas

handful of fresh flat leaf parsley, roughly chopped

pinch of sea salt and black pepper

Heat the oil in a large pan over a medium heat, then add the onion and asparagus tips. Allow to cook for 2 minutes, then add the courgette and celery to the pan along with the vegetable stock.

Tip in the tomatoes and mixed herbs, and increase the heat to high. Break the spaghetti into small pieces and add to the pan. Cover with a lid and cook for 10 minutes, stirring occasionally.

Stir through the watercress and peas, cooking for a further minute. Scatter over the parsley as you remove the pan from the heat. Season with sea salt and black pepper.

rustic ribollita

serves 2

Traditional Italian ribollita is a hearty and economical dish that uses up kitchen leftovers, including bread. It's somewhere between a stew and a soup, with a chunky yet starchy base and a substantial bite from the cannellini beans. If you've got time to make this the night before you eat it, the flavours will deepen; if you eat it straight away, the dish will be a touch milder, yet still delicious.

3 slices of white bread

800ml (28fl oz/3½ cups) good-quality hot vegetable stock

1 tablespoon olive oil

1 onion, roughly chopped

1 carrot, finely sliced

1 celery stick, sliced

3 cloves of garlic, crushed

4 leaves of cavolo nero (Tuscan kale)

400g (14oz) can chopped tomatoes

235g (8oz) can cannellini beans, rinsed and drained

½ teaspoon dried rosemary

½ teaspoon chilli flakes

pinch of sea salt

Tear the bread into small pieces and place into the jug of vegetable stock to soften.

In a large pan, heat the oil over a medium-high heat. Add the onion, carrot and celery to the pan and cook for 2–3 minutes until the carrot begins to soften.

Add the garlic to the pan. Tear the leafy parts of the cavolo nero and throw them into the pan, discarding the tough stems. Stir-fry for 1 minute.

Tip in the tomatoes and cannellini beans. Pour in the stock and softened bread, along with the rosemary and chilli flakes, bringing to the boil over a high heat. Cook for 10 minutes, stirring frequently.

Remove from the heat and season with sea salt.

crispy potato rosti

serves 2

Rosti represents everything that is wonderful about simple cooking. It's a classic fast food staple which is brilliant on its own or as a side dish. I like to serve one whole rosti as a tear and share, but it can also be made into smaller, individual rosti. No need to peel the potatoes as their skins add depth of flavour with no added effort.

If you don't have time to grate the potatoes by hand, use a food processor.

Rinse the potatoes to ensure they are clean, then grate them onto a clean, dry tea towel.

Add the oil to a medium frying pan and bring to a medium-high heat.

Squeeze out as much liquid from the potatoes as you can, twisting the tea towel as you go. When their moisture has been fully removed, sprinkle over the sea salt and black pepper, combining the mixture into a dense, flat rosti.

Use a spatula to place the rosti into the pan, gently pressing it down. Fry for 5 minutes until golden, then flip and fry for a further 5 minutes on the other side. Serve hot.

2 large baking potatoes, chilled

6 tablespoons sunflower oil

generous pinch of coarse sea salt and black pepper

sweet tomato bruschetta with olive tapenade

serves 2

Bruschetta makes the perfect starter, brunch, or amuse-bouche with a hot, crisp base and a juicy topping. Choose a couple of varieties of tomato and the best-quality extra virgin olive oil you can get hold of. Top with a spoonful of fruity olive lemon tapenade, then sit back and dream of sunny days.

Heat a griddle pan and slice the bread into 2cm (¾in) thick slices. Place each slice onto the griddle pan for 2 minutes on each side.

While the bread is toasting, chop the tomatoes and place them in a bowl. Combine with the olive oil.

To make the tapenade, add the olives, sea salt, and basil to a blender, then squeeze in the lemon juice. Blend until coarsely combined.

Remove the bread from the griddle pan and lay on plates. On each slice, spoon over the tomatoes and top with a teaspoon of tapenade.

1 white French stick

6 plum tomatoes

6 orange-yellow tomatoes

2 tablespoons good-quality extra virgin olive oil

For the tapenade
50g (1¾oz) stoned (pitted) mixed olives

generous pinch of sea salt

handful of fresh basil leaves

½ unwaxed lemon

pitta pizzas

serves 2

Pitta breads make wonderful pizza bases that can be loaded with toppings before being baked until golden. Little hands love to help too!

Get creative with the toppings! Switch tomato purée for my Lemon and almond pesto (see page 147) and experiment with flavoured oils.

Preheat the oven to 220°C/425°F/Gas 7.

Arrange the pitta breads on a baking tray and spread one side with the tomato purée.

Press the mushrooms onto the tomato purée.

Shake off any excess oil from the artichokes and roughly slice them, then lay them onto the pittas.

Scatter over the pine nuts and oregano, then drizzle with oil.

Bake for 10 minutes until the base is golden. Scatter with chopped chillies, rocket leaves, basil leaves and olives to serve.

4 white pitta breads

4 tablespoons tomato purée

4 chestnut (cremini) mushrooms, sliced

2 tablespoons jarred artichokes in olive oil

1 tablespoon pine nuts

½ teaspoon dried oregano

drizzle of olive oil

1 red chilli, deseeded and finely sliced

handful of rocket (arugula) leaves, to serve

handful of basil leaves, to serve

8 pitted black olives, slivered, to serve

satay noodles

serves 2

If you're a lover of peanut butter, this bowl of creamy noodles is designed for you. With the perfect balance of heat, salt, and bitters, you'll have this on your table before you can run out to grab a hot box!

To make the sauce, whisk together the peanut butter, soy sauce, and chilli flakes along with 200ml (7fl oz/ scant 1 cup) cold water in a bowl. Whisk in the lime juice to form a smooth paste.

For the noodles, heat the oil in a wok over a high heat. When the oil is hot, throw in the vegetables and stir-fry for 1–2 minutes. Separate the soft noodles and add them to the wok. Pour in the peanut sauce and stir-fry for a further minute.

Sprinkle over the sesame seeds, coriander, and chilli. Serve immediately.

For the sauce
4 tablespoons smooth peanut butter

2 teaspoons dark soy sauce

1 teaspoon dried chilli flakes

juice of 1 unwaxed lime

For the noodles
1 tablespoon sunflower oil

handful of sugar snap peas, halved

1 small carrot, finely sliced

2 spring onions (scallions), chopped

2 packs of soft ready-to-wok noodles (egg free)

2 teaspoons white sesame seeds

small handful of fresh coriander (cilantro)

1 red chilli, deseeded and finely sliced

carrot and cardamom falafel

serves 2

I love street food. The sight, the sound, the sizzle, and of course, that intoxicating aroma drawing you in from afar. My favourite street food is falafel, served in a warm flatbread, with preserved lemon, hot sauce and crisp lettuce. When I don't have the time, or inclination, to go out and grab my street food fix, I make these falafel, with a twist on the classic recipe.

For the speediest result, blitz the falafel ingredients in a food processor or blender, if you don't have one, mash by hand (with some elbow grease).

Heat the oil in a deep pan over a medium-high heat while you prepare the falafel.

Add the chickpeas to a food processor along with the carrot, onion, and red chilli and blitz to a coarse paste.

Add in the garlic, cumin, cardamom, coriander, sea salt, and 2 tablespoons cold water and blitz again until you have a smoother paste.

Spoon out tablespoon-sized amounts of the mixture and roll into about 8 balls. Add to the hot oil using tongs and cook for 1–2 minutes on each side until golden.

In the meantime, lay the lettuce on the flatbreads and place the falafel in when cooked. Top with the houmous, then fold the wrap.

200ml (7fl oz/scant 1 cup) sunflower oil, for shallow-frying

For the falafel
240g (8½oz) can chickpeas (garbanzo beans), rinsed and drained

1 large carrot, roughly chopped

1 onion, roughly chopped

1 small red chilli, deseeded

1 clove of garlic

2 teaspoons ground cumin

½ teaspoon ground cardamom

30g (1oz) bunch of fresh coriander (cilantro), stalks included, roughly chopped

generous pinch of sea salt

For the wraps
2 handfuls of iceberg lettuce

2 flatbreads

2 tablespoons houmous

pea and garden mint fritters

serves 2

Everyone will love these simple fritters as they are bursting with the fresh flavours of pea and mint and are ready in under 10 minutes.

Freshly podded peas give the ultimate burst of flavour to these fritters, however, you can use frozen peas if fresh peas are not available or in season.

Heat the oil in a frying pan over a medium heat while you make the fritter batter.

Mix the flour, baking powder, salt, and mixed herbs in a bowl, then stir through the peas and mint.

Pour in 100ml (3½oz/ scant ½ cup) cold water and stir through to form a paste. Add tablespoon-sized amounts of the batter to the hot pan and cook for 2–3 minutes on each side. Serve hot.

6 tablespoons sunflower oil

For the fritters
120g (4½oz/1 cup) plain (all-purpose) flour

2 teaspoons baking powder

½ teaspoon salt

½ teaspoon dried mixed herbs

6 tablespoons peas (defrosted if frozen)

6 fresh mint leaves, finely chopped

orange, pomegranate, and pistachio pilaf

serves 2

This three-step rice dish is perfect for sharing and can be served hot or cold, making it the perfect lunch or sharing dish. It has layers of flavour, colour, and textures amongst the humble basmati rice.

2 tablespoons olive oil

1 red onion, finely chopped

250g (9oz/1¼ cups) extra-long-grain basmati rice

600ml (20fl oz/2½ cups) hot vegetable stock

2 teaspoons harissa paste

1 teaspoon ground cumin

1 teaspoon ground turmeric

1 pomegranate

1 unwaxed orange

handful of shelled pistachios

generous handful of fresh flat-leaf parsley

pinch of sea salt

In a large pan, heat the oil over a medium heat. Add the onion to the pan and cook for 2 minutes until softened but not browned.

Add in the rice and coat in the onion oil mixture. Pour in the vegetable stock and increase the heat to medium-high.

Spoon in the harissa, cumin, and turmeric and cook for 10 minutes until the stock has absorbed, stirring frequently to prevent sticking.

In the meantime, halve the pomegranate and scoop out the seeds, reserving them in a bowl. Halve the orange and roughly chop the pistachios and parsley.

Remove the pilaf from the heat and stir through the pomegranate seeds, pistachios, and parsley. Squeeze over the orange juice. Season with sea salt.

sweet jacket potatoes with yoghurt, pomegranate, and toasted walnuts

serves 2

Everyone loves an oven-baked jacket potato. That savoury–sweet taste is a true home comfort, however, there are times when you need that comfort fast. I love making sweet jacket potatoes in the microwave; brushing the skin with a little olive oil helps to crisp them up, and their lingering sweetness is reminiscent of that of an oven-baked spud. Load with your favourite toppings, or with mine, which are yoghurt, pomegranate, and walnuts.

2 large sweet potatoes

2 teaspoons olive oil

2 tablespoons walnuts

1 pomegranate

generous handful of fresh flat-leaf parsley, finely chopped

4 tablespoons unsweetened soya yoghurt

pinch of sea salt

Thoroughly wash and dry the sweet potatoes. Brush the skins with the oil, then cook together in an 850W microwave for 8–9 minutes, until a knife can pierce through the filling effortlessly.

While the sweet potatoes are cooking, add the walnuts to a dry pan and toast over a high heat for 2–3 minutes, then set aside.

Slice the pomegranate and gently remove the seeds.

Remove the cooked sweet potatoes from the microwave and carefully slice them down the centre. Generously spoon in the yoghurt and scatter over the toasted walnuts, pomegranate, and parsley. Season with sea salt.

tempura vegetables with a soy, chilli, and coriander dipping sauce

serves 4

People often consider tempura a difficult dish to create, however, it is in fact incredibly easy, with just a few simple ingredients required. The trick to creating the perfect light yet crispy batter is using sparkling, carbonated water that is ice cold. Use vegetables that need minimal preparation, such as button mushrooms and broccoli, to save time.

The dipping sauce can be made in advance and refrigerated in a sealed container for up to three days.

Heat the oil in a deep pan over a high heat while you prepare the vegetables.

Trim the end of the broccoli and slice away the top end of the baby carrots. Remove the very top and bottom of the radishes. Brush the mushrooms to ensure they are dirt free.

Now make the batter. In a wide bowl, mix together the flour, cornflour, and baking powder before whisking in the ice-cold sparkling water. Whisk gently until just smooth. Dip in the vegetables and ensure they are evenly coated in batter, shaking off any excess.

Using a slotted spoon, carefully add half the vegetables to the hot oil and cook for 2–3 minutes. Try not to overfill the pan with the vegetables, as they will stick together. When the batter has puffed up, carefully remove the tempura from the pan and drain on kitchen paper (paper towel), then add the rest of the vegetables to the pan, again cooking for 2–3 minutes.

In the meantime, make the dipping sauce. Pour the passata, soy sauce, maple syrup, chilli flakes, and coriander into a bowl. Cut the lime in half and squeeze in the juice through a sieve to stop any pips going into the bowl. Whisk until combined.

Serve the tempura immediately with individual bowls of dipping sauce.

200ml (7fl oz/scant 1 cup) sunflower oil, for frying

For the vegetables
8 spears of tenderstem broccoli

8 baby carrots

8 radishes

12 button mushrooms

For the batter
150g (5½oz/generous 1 cup) plain (all-purpose) flour

100g (3½oz/¾ cup) cornflour (cornstarch)

1 teaspoon baking powder

200ml (7fl oz/scant 1 cup) ice-cold sparkling water

For the soy, chilli, and coriander dipping sauce
200g (7oz/¾ cup) passata

2 tablespoons soy sauce

1 tablespoon maple syrup

½ teaspoon dried chilli flakes

handful of fresh coriander (cilantro), finely chopped

1 lime

edamame, lime, and sesame jar salad

serves 1

This is a make-now-and-enjoy-later salad that looks as pretty as it tastes. This salad combines flavours of the East, including edamame, coriander, and lime for a refreshing lunch.

Glass jars are great for storing and transporting salads and snacks, perfect to store your made-in-advance creations. They look great too!

Add the edamame beans to a pan and pour over boiling water. Cook over a high heat for 4 minutes, then drain. Rinse in cold water to cool them down.

Add the carrot to the jar as a base layer and sprinkle over the coriander.

Add the cucumber over the coriander layer, then the tomatoes.

Spoon in the edamame beans and press them down gently.

Halve the avocado, remove the stone and peel it. Finely chop the flesh and add it to the jar. Squeeze over the lime juice.

Top with the spinach leaves – this way they will stay crisp without any moisture from the other vegetables. Sprinkle with the sesame seeds and place the lid on the jar. Refrigerate until you wish to eat the salad, then simply shake the jar to coat the salad in the lime juice.

2 tablespoons frozen edamame beans

1 carrot, grated

small handful of fresh coriander (cilantro)

5cm (2in) piece of cucumber, finely sliced

6 cherry tomatoes, halved

1 avocado

juice of 1 unwaxed lime

small handful of baby spinach leaves

1 teaspoon sesame seeds

caramelized fig and pistachio salad

serves 2

Sweet, caramelized figs, salty sundried tomatoes, and earthy pistachio nuts make this impressive salad. Serve while the figs are warm for an elegant dish.

1 tablespoon fig jam

4 fresh figs, halved

1 generous handful of lamb's lettuce

1 generous handful of watercress

2 sundried tomatoes in oil

1 tablespoon shelled pistachio nuts

drizzle of good-quality extra virgin olive oil

Heat a griddle pan over a medium heat. Brush a little fig jam over the cut half of each fig and carefully place cut-side down onto the griddle pan for 2 minutes, then remove from the heat.

In the meantime, arrange the lamb's lettuce and watercress on a serving plate.

Shake off any excess oil from the sundried tomatoes and roughly slice. Scatter onto the leaves along with the pistachios.

Use tongs to place the caramelized figs onto the bed of salad and drizzle with oil just before serving.

beetroot and pickled walnut salad with minted yoghurt

serves 2

The earthy flavours of beetroot and pickled walnuts are brought together with a fresh and creamy vegan minted yoghurt dressing in this simple salad.

You'll find pre-cooked beetroot in vacuum-sealed packs in all supermarkets, which will save you lots of preparation and cooking time.

2 generous handfuls of rocket (arugula)

4 pre-cooked beetroot (beet), finely sliced

2 tablespoons pickled walnuts, drained of excess vinegar

handful of fresh flat-leaf parsley

For the minted yoghurt
2 fresh mint leaves, finely chopped

4 tablespoons unsweetened soya yoghurt

pinch of sea salt

Lay out the rocket on a large serving plate. Lay the beetroot onto the bed of rocket. Spoon over the pickled walnuts and tear over the parsley.

To make the minted yoghurt, add the mint to a bowl with the soya yoghurt and sea salt. Stir to combine.

Spoon the yoghurt over the salad and serve immediately.

squash and orange salad with hazelnuts

serves 2

This salad will keep you warm in cooler months, with fiery ginger, sweet squash, and crunchy hazelnuts.

Blast the butternut squash in a microwave for 2–3 minutes to soften the skin and make peeling and chopping easy and fast.

Heat the oil in a large wok over a medium-high heat. Add the butternut squash to the wok and cook for 5 minutes.

In the meantime, peel the courgette into strips using a vegetable peeler. Add it to the pan with the ginger and sugar snap peas and cook for a further 5 minutes, stirring frequently to avoid burning.

While the vegetables are cooking, arrange the avocado and coriander on a large plate with the watercress and hazelnuts.

To make the dressing, add the oil to a bowl, then slice the orange in half and squeeze in the juice through a sieve. Whisk in the mustard until fully combined.

Place the hot vegetables over the watercress salad and drizzle over the dressing. Serve hot.

2 tablespoons sunflower oil

½ butternut squash, peeled and chopped into small, even chunks

1 courgette (zucchini)

1cm (½in) piece of ginger, peeled and grated

100g (3½oz) sugar snap peas

1 avocado, peeled and chopped

handful of fresh coriander (cilantro), roughly chopped

2 generous handfuls of watercress

handful of hazelnuts

For the dressing
4 tablespoons extra virgin olive oil

1 unwaxed orange

1 teaspoon wholegrain mustard

grilled baby gem, asparagus, and petits pois salad

serves 2

This light salad is as delicious as it is simple. Baby gem lettuce takes on a sweeter, charred flavour once grilled – which is beautiful with the warm, crisp texture. In spring, I like to enjoy this salad with Jersey Royal potatoes, known for their waxy texture and naturally salty flavour.

The lemon and mint dressing will last in a sealed jar for two to three days.

1 tablespoon olive oil

8 spears of asparagus

2 baby gem lettuces

4 tablespoons petits pois (defrosted if frozen)

For the dressing
2 unwaxed lemons

small handful of fresh mint leaves

1 teaspoon Dijon mustard

200ml (7fl oz/scant 1 cup) good-quality extra virgin olive oil

pinch of sea salt and black pepper

Heat the olive oil in a griddle pan over a medium-high heat.

Trim the tough stalks from the asparagus and place the tender spears onto the griddle pan, cooking for 4 minutes on each side.

In the meantime, prepare the dressing by cutting the lemons in half and squeezing the juice through a sieve into a jar. Finely chop the mint and place into the jar along with the mustard. Pour in the extra virgin olive oil, then place a lid on the jar. Shake until combined, then season.

When the asparagus has softened, remove it. Chop each baby gem lettuce in half, removing any tough stalks. Place flat-side down onto the hot griddle pan and add the petits pois, heating for 1 minute until the lettuce appears warm and slightly charred.

Serve the grilled baby gem lettuce with the petits pois, asparagus, and a generous drizzle of the dressing.

mains

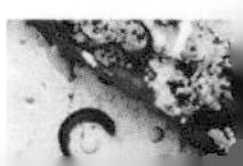

butternut squash and sage macaroni
pasta arrabbiata
balsamic tomato and red onion tarte
harissa aubergine kebabs with cucumber, red onion, and mint relish
vegetable box pie with butter bean mash
sweet and sour with cashews
tuscan bean gnocchi
courgette and lemon pappardelle with pine nuts
one-pot chilli with cinnamon
black bean, sweetcorn, and avocado quesadillas
rainbow chard, red bean, and peanut stew
yasai miso ramen
kerala cauliflower curry
chickpea, apricot, and maple pan-tagine
sweet-stuffed ramiro peppers with salted lemon yoghurt
mediterranean cassoulet
mushroom and ale stroganoff
pad thai jay with lime and sesame
piri-piri bean grill
field mushroom and red pepper fajitas

butternut squash and sage macaroni

serves 2 generously

One of the most popular recipes on my website is a twice-baked butternut macaroni. It's also one of my favourite comfort foods. After having a craving for this slow-cooked dish, but being too hungry to wait, I recreated this creamy classic, which can be in your bowl within 15 minutes.

To cook the butternut squash in the fastest time, ensure it is ripe and chopped into small, even pieces.

Bring a large saucepan of water to the boil. Carefully add the squash to the water and cook over a medium heat for 10–11 minutes until very soft, then drain.

Place the macaroni in a separate saucepan and cover with boiling water. Bring to the boil, then reduce the heat and simmer for 10 minutes until al dente. Drain and keep warm.

Heat the oil in a frying pan and add the onion and garlic. Sprinkle over the sage, then cook over a medium heat for 2–3 minutes until softened but not browned.

Spoon the onion, garlic, and sage mixture into a blender or food processor, along with the butternut squash. Pour in the vegetable stock and blend on high until completely smooth.

Pour the smooth sauce over the macaroni and stir through thoroughly. Season with sea salt and black pepper and garnish with basil.

1 small butternut squash, peeled and chopped into small, even pieces

200g (7oz) dried macaroni (egg free)

1 tablespoon olive oil

1 medium onion, finely chopped

2 cloves of garlic, crushed

2 teaspoons dried sage

400ml (14fl oz/1¾ cups) hot vegetable stock

generous pinch of coarse sea salt and black pepper

small handful of fresh basil, to garnish

pasta arrabbiata

serves 2

A bowl of pasta arrabbiata is one of life's true pleasures – simple, flavoursome, and with a gentle warmth of chilli. Many people are afraid to make their own pasta sauce, but this recipe is so easy, using store-cupboard (pantry) essentials, you'll never go back to the jarred counterpart again!

Dried chilli flakes give a slower, sweeter warmth than fresh chillies, which is perfect for this sauce, and quicker with no chopping required.

Heat the oil in a pan over a medium-high heat and add the oregano, thyme, and chilli flakes. Once they have infused in the oil, then add the garlic and cook for 1 minute.

Tip in the tomatoes and vinegar. Stir through thoroughly and cook for 10 minutes until bubbling and thickened, stirring at intervals.

In the meantime, cook the pasta in a pan of boiling water until al dente, then drain.

Spoon the cooked pasta into the sauce and remove from the heat. Stir through to coat the penne, then season with salt and black pepper.

Scatter over the parsley just before serving.

1 tablespoon olive oil

2 teaspoons dried oregano

1 teaspoon dried thyme

2 teaspoons dried chilli flakes

2 cloves of garlic, crushed

400g (14oz) can chopped tomatoes

1 teaspoon balsamic vinegar

160g (5½oz) dried penne pasta (egg free)

pinch of sea salt and black pepper

small handful of fresh flat-leaf parsley, roughly chopped

balsamic tomato and red onion tarte

serves 4

This six-ingredient recipe is the perfect dish to share at the family table or take to a summer barbecue. Bake the pastry and the filling separately to avoid that dreaded soggy bottom and speed up the cooking time. It's sweet, tangy, and so simple to make.

Many shop-bought puff pastries are vegan friendly as they are made with oil rather than dairy butter. Check the label before you buy. Keep a pack in the freezer, ready to make this quick tarte.

1 sheet of ready-made puff pastry (ensure dairy free)

1 tablespoon olive oil

1 red onion, roughly chopped

300g (10oz) plum tomatoes, halved

3 tablespoons balsamic vinegar

handful of fresh basil leaves

Preheat the oven to 220°C/425°F/Gas 7.

Place the pastry sheet onto a baking tray. Fold over each of the four sides to form a crust, then prick all over the centre with a fork. Bake for 11–12 minutes until golden.

In the meantime, heat the oil in a pan over a medium heat, then add the onion.

Add the tomatoes to the pan, increase the heat to medium-high, and cook for 8 minutes until the onion has softened slightly, stirring frequently.

Spoon in the vinegar and cook for a further 3 minutes until it has reduced and the onion and tomatoes are coated.

Remove the golden pastry from the oven. Spoon over the balsamic tomatoes and onion. Scatter with the basil. Serve hot or allow to cool.

harissa aubergine kebabs with cucumber, red onion, and mint relish

serves 2 generously

These spicy, sweet, and satisfyingly sticky kebabs are made for summer. Simply grill or barbecue! Serve in soft flatbreads with the tangy relish and jewel-like pomegranate seeds and a generous drizzle of tahini.

Once exclusive to Middle-Eastern grocery shops, harissa is now available in most large supermarkets – simply check out the world-food aisle.

1 large aubergine (eggplant), cut into 3cm (1¼in) chunks

6 whole cherry tomatoes

2 tablespoons harissa paste

1 tablespoon maple syrup

2 large flatbreads

1 small pomegranate, seeds only

generous drizzle of tahini paste

For the relish
¼ small cucumber, finely chopped

1 small red onion, finely chopped

handful of fresh mint leaves, roughly chopped

1 tablespoon cider vinegar

Heat a griddle pan over a medium-high heat. Thread the aubergine chunks and cherry tomatoes onto two metal or pre-soaked wooden skewers.

Whisk the harissa paste and maple syrup into a large bowl, then dip the skewers into the mixture, generously coating the aubergine and tomatoes. Place the skewers onto the griddle pan for 5–6 minutes, then turn on the other side and cook for a further 5 minutes.

In the meantime, prepare the relish. Put the cucumber and red onion in a small bowl and stir through the mint. Sprinkle over the vinegar and allow to infuse while the kebabs are cooking.

Arrange the grilled flatbreads on a platter and liberally sprinkle over the pomegranate seeds. Carefully remove the kebabs from the griddle pan and slide off the vegetables onto the flatbreads. Spoon over the relish and tahini and serve immediately.

vegetable box pie with butter bean mash

serves 2

This simple and delicious pie is designed to use up the stray vegetables at the bottom of your veg box or refrigerator. Toss them all into the herb-infused sauce, then layer over the creamy butter bean mash for a fifteen-minute main that will become a firm favourite. For the creamiest mash, source jarred butter beans instead of canned. If canned butter beans are your only option, soak them for a few minutes in boiling water to break down the skins.

Chop the vegetables finely for the fastest cooking time, or slice through a food processor for extra-fast preparation.

Start by making the pie filling. Heat the oil in a pan over a medium heat. Add the leek, carrots, and celery to the pan and soften for 2 minutes. Throw the mushrooms and chard into the pan and sauté for a further 2 minutes.

Add the garlic and pour in the red wine. Scatter over the rosemary and thyme and reduce for 1 minute. Pour in the passata and loosely cover with a lid. Cook down for 10 minutes.

While the pie filling is cooking, prepare the butter bean mash. In a wide pan, heat the oil and cook the garlic over a low-medium heat for 1 minute. Add the butter beans to the pan and stir frequently for 3–4 minutes until the beans have heated through and are coated in olive oil and garlic.

Remove the butter bean pan from the heat and stir in the lemon juice. Mash down until semi-smooth, then season with sea salt.

Remove the other pan from the heat and divide the mixture into two pie dishes. Top with the butter bean mash and serve hot.

For the filling
1 tablespoon olive oil

1 small leek, finely chopped

2 carrots, finely chopped

1 celery stick, finely chopped

4 chestnut (cremini) mushrooms, chopped

handful of chard leaves, chopped

2 cloves of garlic, crushed

3 tablespoons red wine (ensure vegan)

1 teaspoon dried rosemary

½ teaspoon dried thyme

400g (1lb/1¾ cups) passata

generous pinch of sea salt

For the butter bean mash
1 tablespoon olive oil

1 clove of garlic, crushed

600g (1¼lb) butter beans (lima), drained and rinsed

juice of ½ an unwaxed lemon

generous pinch of sea salt

sweet and sour with cashews

serves 2

Try the takeaway challenge and have this classic dish on your table in less time than it can be delivered to your door! Serve generously with Edamame fried rice (see page 150).

Fresh pineapple really lifts this dish. Take slices from a whole fruit or buy the pre-chopped variety from the chilled section in the supermarket.

To make the sauce, whisk together the sugar, vinegar, ketchup, and soy sauce in a medium pan until combined. Stir in the pineapple chunks, then cook over a medium heat for 10 minutes until bubbling.

While the sauce is cooking, work on the vegetables. Heat the oil in a wok over a medium-high heat. Add the red pepper and radishes to the wok, along with the mangetout and baby corns and stir-fry for 3–4 minutes.

Add the spring onions and cashew nuts to the wok, stir-frying for a further minute, then remove the wok from the heat.

Pour over the sweet-and-sour sauce and stir through. Serve hot.

For the sweet-and-sour sauce
50g (1¾oz/¼ cup) soft brown sugar

25ml (5 teaspoons) malt vinegar

150g (5½oz/1¼ cups) tomato ketchup

1 tablespoon light soy sauce

200g (7oz/1 cup) pineapple chunks

For the vegetables
1 tablespoon sunflower oil

1 red (bell) pepper, finely sliced

6 radishes, finely sliced

10 mangetout (snow peas)

10 baby corns

2 spring onions (scallions), finely chopped

3 tablespoons cashew nuts

tuscan bean gnocchi

serves 4

Imagine a faded copper pan, with a rustic casserole bubbling over the side, filled with pillows of potato gnocchi – you'd never guess such a hearty dish could be ready in 15 minutes. Gnocchi are a useful storecupboard (pantry) essential and available from most supermarkets – just check that they are egg free. This really is comfort food at its best.

Heat the oil in a large pan over a medium heat. Add the onion and celery to the pan and allow to soften for 2 minutes.

Add the yellow pepper and garlic to the pan, along with the rosemary, oregano, and thyme, cooking for a further minute.

Tip in the tomatoes, then the borlotti beans. Stir through the balsamic vinegar and yeast extract. Increase the heat to high and cook for 10 minutes, stirring frequently.

Once the sauce has started to reduce down and combine, add the gnocchi and cook for 2 minutes to heat through. Season with salt and black pepper and scatter with basil leaves just before serving.

2 tablespoons olive oil

1 onion, finely sliced

1 celery stick, finely chopped

1 yellow (bell) pepper, sliced

1 clove of garlic, crushed

1 teaspoon dried rosemary

1 teaspoon dried oregano

½ teaspoon dried thyme

400g (14oz) can chopped tomatoes

235g (8oz) can borlotti beans, rinsed and drained

1 tablespoon balsamic vinegar

1 teaspoon yeast extract

500g (1lb 2oz) gnocchi (egg free)

generous pinch of sea salt and black pepper

generous handful of fresh basil leaves

courgette and lemon pappardelle with pine nuts

serves 2 generously

This fresh, lemony pasta tastes like summer in a bowl, even when it's cold outside. The grassy flavour of courgette meets the crisp bites of toasted pine nuts, all brought together by addictively slippery pappardelle ribbons.

Use a good-quality extra virgin olive oil to dress the pasta, as a quick way to add a light flavour.

200g (7oz) dried pappardelle (egg free)

1 tablespoon olive oil

1 onion, finely chopped

1 clove of garlic, crushed

2 medium courgettes (zucchini), grated

1 tablespoon pine nuts

2 unwaxed lemons

generous pinch of sea salt and black pepper

2 tablespoons extra virgin olive oil

handful of fresh basil leaves

Cook the pappardelle in a large saucepan of boiling water over a high-medium heat for 10 minutes until al dente, then drain.

In the meantime, heat the olive oil in a large frying pan over a low-medium heat. Add the onion to the pan, followed by the garlic. Add the courgettes to the pan and increase the heat to medium. Stir frequently to avoid burning and encourage even cooking, and cook for 4–5 minutes. Add the pine nuts and cook for a further minute.

While the courgette is cooking, slice the lemons in half. When the courgettes have softened, squeeze over the juice of each lemon through a sieve, then remove the pan from the heat and season with sea salt and black pepper.

Toss the cooked, drained pappardelle into the courgette and coat evenly. Drizzle with extra virgin olive oil and scatter over basil leaves. Serve immediately.

one-pot chilli with cinnamon

serves 2 generously

Warming, homely, and comforting – nothing beats a home-cooked chilli, especially one that is ready in 15 minutes. There's nothing technical about this recipe: chop the vegetables roughly and let the chilli bubble away and cook itself. The not-so-secret ingredient of cinnamon will lift this chilli to new flavour levels, with a subtle sweetness among the smoky ingredients.

Heating chopped tomatoes in the pan will create a hot base for your vegetables, reducing the overall cooking time of the chilli.

Tip the tomatoes into a heavy-based saucepan over a medium heat. Add the onion, celery and red pepper to the pan and increase the heat to high.

Add the kidney beans and sweetcorn to the pan.

Spoon in the chilli powder, paprika, cinnamon, ketchup, and yeast extract and allow to cook through for 10 minutes, stirring frequently to avoid burning the base.

When the vegetables in the chilli have softened, remove the pan from the heat. Scatter over the avocado and parsley, and squeeze over the lime juice through a sieve. Season with smoked sea salt.

400g (14oz) can chopped tomatoes

1 onion, roughly chopped

1 celery stick, chopped

1 red (bell) pepper, deseeded and sliced

240g (8½oz) can red kidney beans, rinsed and drained

3 tablespoons frozen or canned sweetcorn

2 teaspoons chilli powder

1 teaspoon smoked paprika

½ teaspoon ground cinnamon

1 tablespoon tomato ketchup

1 teaspoon yeast extract

1 avocado, peeled, stoned and sliced

handful of fresh flat-leaf parsley, roughly chopped

½ unwaxed lime

pinch of smoked sea salt

black bean, sweetcorn, and avocado quesadillas

serves 2

These pockets of flavour are fast and satisfying with a crispy outer and a hot, saucy middle. Perfect as an end-of-the-month meal when you're using up what's in your storecupboard (pantry). Feel free to add some dairy-free cheese, although you'll find the avocado is creamy and delicious enough.

Soft tortillas freeze successfully and take only minutes to defrost.

1 small red onion, finely chopped

1 avocado, peeled, stoned and finely chopped

2 tablespoons sweetcorn (defrosted if frozen)

400g (14oz) can black beans, rinsed and drained

3 tablespoons barbecue sauce (ensure vegan)

pinch of sea salt

1 tablespoon sunflower oil

4 soft tortillas

1 unwaxed lime, quartered

Mix the red onion, avocado, and sweetcorn in a bowl.

Add the black beans to the bowl and spoon in the barbecue sauce. Stir to combine evenly and season with a pinch of salt.

Heat the oil in a griddle pan over a medium heat while you prepare the quesadillas. Lay out two of the tortillas and spread the black bean mixture over each one. Lay the remaining two tortillas over the topped ones and press down.

Carefully place a quesadilla into the pan and cook for 3–4 minutes on each side. Remove using tongs and set aside to keep warm. Repeat for the second quesadilla.

Slice the quesadillas into quarters and squeeze the lime juice over to taste.

rainbow chard, red bean, and peanut stew

serves 4

This is soul food in a bowl. It's creamy and rich with a subtle heat. Rainbow chard adds a pretty array of colours to the stew, but if you don't have any available, you can substitute it for Swiss chard or spring greens. Don't leave out the coriander topping at the end, as this lifts the stew with its fresh flavour. This is one of my favourite foods to eat on a cold, autumn day, while wearing a cosy, knitted jumper.

If you don't eat all the stew, simply add in some vegetable stock and whizz until smooth in a blender for a fast soup the following day.

Heat the oil in a large pan over a high heat. Add the onion and rainbow chard to the pan and sauté for 2 minutes until the onion begins to soften.

Add the garlic to the pan, along with the chilli flakes, cumin, and ginger and cook for a further minute.

Tip in the tomatoes and spoon in the peanut butter. Reduce the heat to medium.

Add the red kidney beans and soy sauce to the pan. Stir regularly to prevent burning and cook for 8 minutes.

Spoon into bowls and scatter with the coriander. Season with salt.

1 tablespoon sunflower oil

1 onion, roughly chopped

100g (3½oz) rainbow chard, roughly chopped

3 cloves of garlic, crushed

1 teaspoon dried chilli flakes

1 teaspoon ground cumin

½ teaspoon ground ginger

400g (14oz) can chopped tomatoes

4 rounded tablespoons crunchy peanut butter

240g (8½oz) can red kidney beans, rinsed and drained

1 tablespoon light soy sauce

generous handful of fresh coriander (cilantro), roughly chopped

pinch of sea salt

yasai miso ramen

serves 2

This is the ultimate meal in bowl. 'Yasai' is the Japanese word for vegetable. In this dish, vegetables are simmered with ramen noodles in a fragrant stock, seasoned with white miso. You can find miso in many supermarkets and health-food shops – I find that white miso has a milder flavour than red or mixed pastes. Pile your bowl up high!

Heat the oil in a large pan over a medium-high heat. Add the garlic and ginger to the pan, along with the chopped chilli.

Pour in the hot water and stir through the white miso paste. Sprinkle in the Chinese five spice and star anise and bring to the boil for 5 minutes.

While the stock is cooking, remove the star anise. Add the carrot, red pepper, pak choi, and broccoli to the pan. Add the dried ramen noodles and cook for 5–6 minutes until the vegetables are bright and the noodles have softened.

Remove the pan from the heat and ladle into bowls. Scatter with the spring onions and coriander, and squeeze over the lime juice. Sprinkle with the sesame seeds and sliced red chilli and serve.

1 tablespoon sunflower oil

2 cloves of garlic, grated

2cm (¾in) piece of ginger, peeled and grated

1 red chilli, finely chopped

600ml (20fl oz/2½ cups) hot water

1 rounded teaspoon white miso paste

½ teaspoon Chinese five spice

2 whole star anise

1 carrot, finely sliced

1 red (bell) pepper, finely sliced

6 leaves of pak choi (bok choy), finely sliced

6 florets of tenderstem broccoli

150g (5½oz) dried ramen noodles (egg free)

2 spring onions (scallions), finely chopped

handful of fresh coriander (cilantro), finely chopped

juice of 1 unwaxed lime

1 tablespoon white sesame seeds

1 red chilli, deseeded and finely sliced

kerala cauliflower curry

serves 2 generously

Cauliflower makes a fantastic curry ingredient, as its gentle flavour allows for all the spices to infuse through it, so every bite is as delicious as the next. This dish has a delicate blend of spices, which you can adjust to your own preferences.

You can find cooked Puy lentils in ready-to-use packs available from most supermarkets, making them a super-speedy addition to this flavoursome curry.

2 tablespoons sunflower oil

2 onions, finely chopped

1 red fresh chilli, finely chopped

2cm (¾in) piece of ginger, peeled and finely chopped

3 cloves of garlic, crushed

1 tablespoon ground turmeric

2 teaspoons garam masala

2 teaspoons ground cumin

1 teaspoon cumin seeds

400ml (14fl oz) can full-fat coconut milk

150ml (5fl oz/⅔ cup) hot water

1 small cauliflower, cut into bite-size florets

2 large flatbreads (optional)

200g (7oz/3 cups) cooked Puy lentils

handful of fresh coriander (cilantro), roughly chopped

generous pinch of sea salt

½ fresh red chilli, finely sliced

Heat the oil in a large pan over a medium heat. Add the onions, chilli, and ginger to the pan and cook for 2–3 minutes until the onions soften but do not brown. Add the garlic, then stir through the turmeric, garam masala, ground cumin, and cumin seeds, cooking for a further minute.

Pour in the coconut milk and hot water and allow to simmer. Add the cauliflower to the pan and cook for 5–6 minutes, then increase the heat to medium-high until the cauliflower is al dente.

Grill the flatbreads, if using, for one minute on each side in a griddle plan. Tip the lentils into the pan and stir through. Remove the pan from the heat and scatter with the coriander, sea salt and extra chilli just before serving.

chickpea, apricot, and maple pan-tagine

serves 4

My favourite meal is a two-hour slow-cooked tagine; the sweet fragrances escaping from the tagine pot always entice me in. When I crave tagine but only have 15 minutes to spare, I love this colourful and flavourful recipe. Serve with my Sweet-stuffed Ramiro peppers (see opposite page) and Caramelized red onion houmous (see page 153).

You can make up this spice mix in advance and store it in a sealed jar, or alternatively, purchase a pre-blended spice mix called ras-el-hanout.

Add the oil, cumin, paprika, turmeric, and cinnamon into a large pan and infuse over a medium heat for 1 minute.

Add the sweet potato, onion, and green beans to the pan. Increase the heat to high and sauté the vegetables in the spice mix for 2 minutes. Add the garlic and ginger and cook for a further minute.

Pour in the stock and bring to the boil, then reduce the heat to medium, simmering for 10 minutes. Add the chickpeas to the pan, along with the apricots and maple syrup and loosely cover with a lid.

When the sweet potato has softened, remove the pan from the heat and stir in the parsley. Chop the lemon in half, then squeeze in the juice through a sieve. Season with salt.

2 tablespoons olive oil

2 teaspoons ground cumin

1 teaspoon paprika

1 teaspoon ground turmeric

½ teaspoon ground cinnamon

1 large sweet potato, peeled and cut into small chunks

1 red onion, roughly chopped

2 generous handfuls of green beans, topped and tailed

2 cloves of garlic, crushed

2cm (¾in) piece of ginger, peeled and grated

300ml (10fl oz/1¼ cups) hot vegetable stock

240g (8½oz) can chickpeas (garbanzo beans), rinsed and drained

6 dried apricots

1 tablespoon maple syrup

generous handful of fresh flat-leaf parsley, torn

1 unwaxed lemon

generous pinch of sea salt

sweet-stuffed ramiro peppers with salted lemon yoghurt

serves 2

Try to source Ramiro peppers as they have a thinner skin than regular bell peppers, so they roast faster with a sweet, smoky taste.

Preheat the oven to 200°C/400°F/Gas 6.

Heat the oil in a pan over a low heat. Add the onion to the pan and fry for 10 minutes until browned.

Chop the top off the peppers and slice in half lengthways, removing the seeds and inner stem. Place on a baking tray and roast for 10 minutes until the edges have darkened.

In the meantime, tip the couscous into a small bowl with the hot vegetable stock. Cover with a lid and allow the stock to absorb over five minutes. When the couscous is light and fluffy, fork through and stir in the parsley and coriander.

Remove the onion from the heat after 10 minutes and spoon in the couscous. Sprinkle in the cinnamon and mixed spice and stir through the sultanas and flaked almonds. Spoon the onion and couscous filling into the peppers and keep warm.

To make the dressing, whisk the yoghurt and salt in a bowl with the lemon juice. Spoon over the stuffed peppers just before serving.

Serve with Caramelized red onion houmous (see page 153) and Chickpea, apricot and maple pan-tagine (see opposite page).

1 tablespoon olive oil

1 onion, finely sliced

6 Ramiro peppers

200g (7oz/1¼ cups) couscous

200ml (7fl oz/scant 1 cup) hot vegetable stock

small handful of fresh flat-leaf parsley, finely chopped

small handful of fresh coriander (cilantro), finely chopped

¼ teaspoon ground cinnamon

¼ teaspoon ground mixed spice

1 tablespoon plump sultanas (golden raisins)

1 tablespoon flaked (slivered) almonds

For the yoghurt dressing
4 tablespoons unsweetened soya yoghurt

pinch of sea salt

juice of ½ unwaxed lemon

mediterranean cassoulet

serves 2

A warming pot that will take you back to hazy, warm summer nights, whatever the weather. Serve with a Crispy potato rosti (see page 56).

1 tablespoon olive oil

1 red onion, roughly chopped

1 yellow (bell) pepper, chopped

1 small courgette (zucchini), diced

2 cloves of garlic, crushed

400g (14oz) can chopped tomatoes

2 tablespoons tomato ketchup

handful of stoned (pitted) black olives

4 sundried tomatoes in oil, drained and roughly sliced

2 teaspoons dried herbes de Provence

1 teaspoon dried oregano

½ unwaxed lemon

pinch of sea salt and black pepper

handful of fresh basil leaves

Heat the oil in a large saucepan over a medium heat, then add the onion and cook for 2 minutes. Throw the yellow pepper and courgette into the pan and cook for 2 minutes, then add the garlic for the final minute.

Tip in the tomatoes and stir through the tomato ketchup, then add the olives.

Add the sundried tomatoes to the cassoulet with the herbes de Provence and oregano. Increase the heat to medium-high for 10 minutes.

When the cassoulet has cooked and the vegetables have softened, remove the pan from the heat and squeeze over the lemon juice through a sieve. Season with salt and black pepper and garnish with fresh basil leaves just before serving.

mushroom and ale stroganoff

serves 2

If you love the earthy, creamy flavours of mushroom stroganoff, you'll love this boozy twist on the classic. As a nod to my Yorkshire roots, I always use a dark ale from a local micro-brewery, but you can simply use your favourite – just check that it's free of any animal ingredients, including isinglass. Serve this stroganoff generously with rice or over pasta.

This is a great recipe for using up ingredients at the back of your refrigerator, including non-dairy yoghurt. Opt for an unsweetened soya yoghurt for the best flavour in this dish, or switch to a non-dairy cream, available from most supermarkets.

Heat the oil in a large pan over a medium heat. Add the onion to the pan and cook for 2–3 minutes until softened but not browned. Add the mushrooms and garlic to the pan and quick-fry over a high heat for 2 minutes.

Pour the ale into the pan and reduce the heat to medium. Add the soy sauce and paprika and allow to cook for 10 minutes until the ale reduces.

Remove the pan from the heat and stir through the soya yoghurt until combined. Season with salt and scatter with parsley just before serving.

1 tablespoon olive oil

1 onion, finely chopped

300g (10oz) chestnut (cremini) mushrooms, sliced

2 cloves of garlic, crushed

200ml (7fl oz/scant 1 cup) vegan ale

1 tablespoon dark soy sauce

1 teaspoon paprika

3 rounded tablespoons unsweetened soya yoghurt

generous pinch of sea salt

generous handful of fresh flat-leaf parsley, roughly chopped

pad thai jay with lime and sesame

serves 2

This is my go-to recipe for when I'm hungry and in a hurry, as it is fast, simple, and totally satisfying. I prefer to use low-preparation, fast-cook vegetables, however, feel free to adapt to what you have at home.

Soft noodles reduce the cooking time of this pad Thai jay, however, do ensure they are vegan as some types may contain egg. You're more likely to find the egg-free versions stored on the shelves rather than in the chiller cabinets.

1 tablespoon sunflower oil

6 florets of long-stem broccoli

generous handful of kale

1 small red chilli, finely chopped

10 sugar snap peas

8 tablespoons light soy sauce

2 packs of soft cooked noodles (egg free)

1 spring onion (scallion), finely sliced

handful of fresh coriander (cilantro), finely chopped

1 tablespoon peanuts, roughly crushed

1 tablespoon white sesame seeds

1 red chilli, deseeded and finely sliced

1 unwaxed lime

Heat the oil in a wok over a high heat until smoking hot.

In the meantime, trim any tough stems from the broccoli and kale.

Add the chilli, broccoli, kale, and sugar snap peas to the wok and stir-fry for 3–4 minutes.

Spoon in the soy sauce and stir through. Then add the noodles and continue to stir-fry for 2–3 minutes, being careful not to break the noodles. Cook until all the ingredients are coated in soy sauce and the vegetables are crisp and bright.

Remove the wok from the heat and stir the spring onion and coriander through the pad Thai jay. Scatter the peanuts over the top along with the sesame seeds and red chilli.

Slice the lime in half and squeeze the juice through a sieve onto the noodles. Serve immediately.

piri-piri bean grill

serves 4

This recipe turns storecupboard (pantry) essentials into something spicy and special that the whole family will love. These baked beans are flavoured with smoky spices and rounds of orange which create an authentic piri-piri flavour. Never skimp on the fresh coriander and lemon, at the end, as they add a fresh edge. Serve generously with sweet potato wedges, for unashamed dipping.

Use a large frying pan for this recipe, so all the ingredients cook evenly. A paella pan is just the ticket!

Heat the oil in a paella pan over a medium-high heat. Add the onion and yellow pepper to the centre of the pan to cook for 2 minutes. Throw in the cherry tomatoes along with the smoked paprika, chilli powder, chilli flakes and oregano.

Add the baked beans with their tomato sauce and the kidney beans to the pan. Stir to combine the vegetables, spices, and beans and simmer while you peel and slice the orange into fine rounds. Lay them into the beans and cook down for 10 minutes, stirring frequently to prevent burning.

When the beans are sizzling and appear fully combined with the spices, remove the pan from the heat. Scatter over the coriander and red chilli, then squeeze over the lemon juice through a sieve. Season with smoked sea salt.

2 tablespoons olive oil

1 red onion, finely sliced into rings

1 yellow (bell) pepper, finely sliced

6 cherry tomatoes

2 teaspoons smoked paprika

½ teaspoon chilli powder

½ teaspoon dried chilli flakes

½ teaspoon dried oregano

2 x 415g (14½oz) cans baked beans in tomato sauce

240g (8½oz) can red kidney beans, rinsed and drained

1 unwaxed orange

generous handful of fresh coriander (cilantro), roughly chopped

1 red chilli, deseeded and finely sliced

1 unwaxed lemon

generous pinch of smoked sea salt

field mushroom and red pepper fajitas

serves 2

These feisty fajitas are a firm weeknight favourite.

The seasoning can be made in advance and stored in an airtight jar away from sunlight to preserve the flavour.

Prepare the fajita seasoning by combining the chilli powder, smoked paprika, garlic powder, ground cumin and salt in a bowl, then set aside.

Heat the oil in a large frying pan or wok over a medium-high heat. When the oil begins to smoke, throw in the onion, red pepper, mushrooms, and celery and stir-fry for 3–4 minutes.

Pour the seasoning mix into the wok and stir through to coat all the vegetables. Continue to stir-fry for 2 minutes, then squeeze over the lime juice through a sieve and remove from the heat.

Arrange the tortillas on a platter and throw on the coriander and lettuce. Pile over the hot, seasoned vegetables and finish with a spoonful of mayonnaise before wrapping and serving.

4 soft tortillas

generous handful of fresh coriander (cilantro), roughly shredded

generous handful of iceberg lettuce, roughly shredded

2 tablespoons egg-free mayonnaise

For the fajita seasoning
1 tablespoon chilli powder

1 teaspoon smoked paprika

½ teaspoon garlic powder

½ teaspoon ground cumin

½ teaspoon sea salt

For the vegetables
2 tablespoons sunflower oil

1 red onion, sliced

1 red (bell) pepper, sliced

2 field mushrooms, sliced

2 celery sticks, sliced

1 unwaxed lime

sweet stuff

traditional sultana scones
chocolate and cherry mug brownie
vanilla rice pudding
banana split ice cream
salted chocolate mousse
plum and almond galette
raspberry, rose, and pistachio crumble
peanut butter blondie flapjacks
bonfire apples
crêpes
lime and coconut syllabub
blackberry mojito
summer punch slushie
spiced rum and cinnamon grilled pineapple with coconut cream
the lazy millionaire's shortbread pudding
syrup sponge pudding
st clement's mince pies
2 minute chocolate chip and pecan cookie
chai tea poached pears
cheat's strawberry balsamic jam

traditional sultana scones

makes about 6 medium scones

Quintessentially British and perfect with a pot of tea, there's little in life that can beat a sultana scone. This recipe is perfect for when unexpected guests turn up, as they are simple to make and quick to cook - and best served warm, straight from the oven.

When using a dough cutter, never twist when removing it as it will result in uneven scones. Simply press down firmly and remove with the dough intact – simple and quick!

Preheat the oven to 220°C/425°F/Gas 7.

In a large mixing bowl, stir together the flour, baking powder, and sugar. Rub in the vegan butter until the mixture resembles breadcrumbs. Stir in the sultanas until coated with flour. Pour in the milk, a little at a time, and work into a smooth dough.

Place the dough on a floured surface. Use your hands to press it out to a to 2cm (¾in) thickness. Using a scone cutter, press through the dough and place the scones onto a greased baking tray. Brush the top of each scone with soya milk.

Bake for 10–11 minutes until the top is golden. Best served warm.

Serve with lashings of jam and fresh fruit.

220g (8oz/1¾ cups) self-raising (self-rising) flour, plus extra for dusting

1 teaspoon baking powder

2 tablespoons caster (superfine) sugar

50g (1¾oz) vegan butter, plus extra for greasing

50g (1¾oz/⅓ cup) sultanas (golden raisins)

120ml (4fl oz/½ cup) soya milk

1 tablespoon extra flour, for pressing and flouring

1 tablespoon extra soya milk, for brushing

chocolate and cherry mug brownie

serves 1

When the need for a warm, gooey brownie arises, add these ingredients into a mug and let your microwave do all the hard work so you don't have to.

Mix the flour, cocoa powder, sugar, and chocolate chips together in a mug.

Stir in the jam, oil, and 2 tablespoons cold water and mix until combined.

Cook in the microwave for 2 minutes, then allow to stand for 1 minute before indulging.

4 tablespoons self-raising (self-rising) flour

2 tablespoons cocoa powder

2 tablespoons caster (superfine) sugar

1 tablespoon dark chocolate chips

2 tablespoons cherry jam

1 tablespoon sunflower oil

vanilla rice pudding

serves 4

Rice pudding doesn't have to be reserved for the days when you've got hours to bake; this stove-top version is fuss free and ready in just 10 minutes. Flaked pudding rice is the magical ingredient here as it cooks so quickly and recreates a pudding that will take you back to childhood teatimes.

In a large pan, heat the rice, soya milk, and sugar over a high heat for 5 minutes, stirring frequently.

Split the vanilla pod lengthways and scrape out the seeds. Scoop them into the pan and stir through. Reduce the heat to medium and simmer for a further 5 minutes until rice pudding has thickened.

100g (3½oz/generous ½ cup) flaked pudding rice

800ml (28fl oz/3½ cups) vanilla-flavoured soya milk

1 tablespoon caster (superfine) sugar

1 vanilla pod (bean)

Vanilla seeds scraped from the whole pod give the sweetest flavour. If you don't have pods available, use a tablespoon of good-quality vanilla paste instead.

banana split ice cream

serves 4

No ice-cream maker? No problem! This recipe combines all the best parts of a classic banana split into a sweet treat that will transport you to retro times. If you like your ice cream full of surprises, this is definitely the recipe for you.

I always keep a few bananas in the freezer to make this ice cream on a whim. Remove the banana skin before freezing (peeling a frozen banana is more difficult than it sounds!) and keep skinned bananas in sealed bags until you need them.

Put the frozen bananas, maple syrup, soya yoghurt, and peanut butter into a high-powered blender or food processer and blitz until completely smooth.

Stir through the pretzels, glacé cherries, flaked almonds, and chocolate chips until combined and serve immediately.

4 frozen bananas

4 tablespoons maple syrup

1 tablespoon vanilla soya yoghurt

1 tablespoon smooth peanut butter

1 tablespoon roughly crushed salted pretzels

1 tablespoon glacé (candied) cherries (ensure carmine free)

2 teaspoons flaked (slivered) almonds

1 teaspoon dark chocolate chips

salted chocolate mousse

serves 4

Imagine an intensely rich mousse, silky smooth with a subtle balance of sweetness and smoked salt. Serve at the end of an exquisite meal, in a bright white espresso cup. Just don't tell anyone it contains avocado.

250g (9oz) good-quality very dark chocolate

1 ripe avocado

3 tablespoons maple syrup

2 tablespoons unsweetened soya milk

1 teaspoon vanilla extract

pinch of smoked sea salt flakes

Break up the chocolate into even pieces and place in a heatproof bowl. Blast for 30 seconds in the microwave, stir, then heat again for a few more seconds until melted.

Cut the avocado in half, remove the stone and scoop out the flesh into a blender. Spoon in the melted chocolate, maple syrup, soya milk, and vanilla extract and blend on high until combined. Use a spatula to scrape the mixture back to the centre of the blades and blend on high again until completely smooth.

Pour into small cups or ramekins, then sprinkle with the smoked sea salt flakes. Chill for 5 minutes before serving.

plum and almond galette

serves 4

Traditionally, a galette is a free-form pastry pie, slow-baked with a fruity filling. Its rustic, home-baked appearance and piping hot fruit topping is an effortless yet impressive addition to any family table. Who'd have thought it could be recreated in just 15 minutes? Your secret is safe with me.

1 sheet of shop-bought shortcrust pastry (ensure vegan)

6 ripe plums

2 tablespoons plum jam

1 tablespoon amaretto liqueur

2 tablespoons flaked (slivered) almonds

Preheat the oven to 220°C/425°F/Gas 7.

Unroll the pastry directly onto a baking tray. Fold over the edges roughly, sealing with a little water if needed. Bake for 10–12 minutes until golden.

In the meantime, prepare the plum filling. Slice each plum in half, remove the stone, then cut each half into four thin slices. Place the sliced plums into a pan with the jam and amaretto liqueur, then bring to the boil over a medium-high heat for 5–6 minutes until bubbling.

In a separate dry pan, toast the almonds over a high heat for 1–2 minutes until golden brown.

Remove the pastry from the oven and carefully spoon in the plum and amaretto filling. Sprinkle over the toasted almonds and serve immediately.

raspberry, rose, and pistachio crumble

serves 4

Crumble is my ultimate pudding. The sweet, baked fruit and crunchy topping makes it the most comforting bowl there is. Always bake the fruit in a separate tray to the topping, then assemble just before serving; that way the crumble topping will stay crunchy and crisp.

Soft fruits cook in super-fast time, so when you're trying different flavour combinations, opt for fast-cook fruits, including clementines, blackberries, rhubarb, and blackcurrants.

Preheat the oven to 200°C/400°F/Gas 6.

Arrange the raspberries on a baking tray and drizzle over the rose extract.

To make the topping, mix together the flour, oats, and sugar in a bowl. Rub in the coconut oil or vegan butter until the mixture resembles breadcrumbs. Roughly chop the pistachios in half and stir into the mixture. Spoon the topping mixture into a separate deep baking tray.

Bake both trays for 10–12 minutes until the fruit is soft and bubbling and the topping is golden. Spoon the fruit into bowls and top generously with the crumble.

300g (10oz/2½ cups) fresh raspberries

1 teaspoon good-quality rose extract

For the topping
100g (3½oz/¾ cup) plain (all-purpose) flour

50g (1¾oz/½ cup) rolled oats

50g (1¾oz/¼ cup) demerara sugar

2 tablespoons coconut oil or vegan butter, at room temperature

2 tablespoons shelled pistachios

peanut butter blondie flapjacks

makes 6

These squidgy, oaty bars are halfway between a blondie and a brownie, with the comforting taste of creamy peanut butter. Add a pinch of coarse sea salt to the top just before baking as an easy way to take these blondie flapjacks from simple to sublime.

100g (3½oz/½ cup) light brown sugar

2 tablespoons vegan butter

6 tablespoons smooth peanut butter

3 tablespoons golden syrup

300g (10oz/3½ cups) rolled oats

pinch of coarse sea salt

Preheat the oven to 180°C/350°F/Gas 4.

Add the sugar, vegan butter, peanut butter, and golden syrup to a medium saucepan and melt over a medium-high heat for 2–3 minutes. Stir often until the butter has melted and all the ingredients have combined. Tip in the oats and stir until all the oats have been coated in the melted mixture.

Press the oaty mixture into a 3cm (1¼in) depth baking tray lined with baking paper and flatten down using the back of a spoon. Crush over the sea salt and bake for 10 minutes until golden.

Remove from the oven and cut into squares. Leave in the baking tray until cool.

bonfire apples

serves 4

Autumn is my favourite season. The crisp, orange leaves, fresh chill in the air, and of course, toffee apples. To make the process fuss free, prepare the apples and nuts before you prepare the sugar, then keep them close by ready for dipping in the molten syrup. No autumnal gathering should be without these sweet, crackling treats.

Use a sugar thermometer for the perfect toffee shell every time.

4 Granny Smith apples

3 tablespoons blanched hazelnuts, roughly chopped

200g (7oz/generous 1 cup) caster (superfine) sugar

1 teaspoon malt or cider vinegar

2 tablespoons golden syrup

Remove the stalks from the apples and push a wooden lollipop stick through the base end of the apples. Place a sheet of greaseproof paper on a baking tray and add the apples. Set aside. Place the hazelnuts in a bowl.

Tip the sugar into a large pan with 50ml (2fl oz/¼ cup) cold water over a medium heat for 5 minutes. When the sugar has dissolved, stir in the vinegar and golden syrup. Place a sugar thermometer into the pan and boil to 'hard-crack' stage, or 150°C (302°F). If you don't have a sugar thermometer, you can test if the toffee is at the hard-crack stage by dropping a spoonful of the mixture into a bowl of cold water – it should become hard and brittle when removed from the water.

When the toffee has reached the right temperature, remove it from the heat and carefully dip each apple into the hot toffee. Lay the coated apples on the greaseproof paper and sprinkle with the hazelnuts, before allowing to firm up for 2–3 minutes.

crêpes

makes about 6

Elegant and simple crêpes are deliciously delicate and perfect to personalize as basic, sweet, or savoury. I like mine sprinkled with a little lavender sugar, folded, then eaten with a fork.

Filling ideas include vegan chocolate hazelnut spread, golden syrup, or mixed berries. Or for something totally different, try them stuffed with Sweet and sour with cashews (see page 88).

2 tablespoons sunflower oil, for frying

For the batter

150g (5½oz/generous 1 cup) plain (all-purpose) flour

250ml (9fl oz/1 cup) almond milk

½ teaspoon caster (superfine) sugar

½ teaspoon fine salt

1 tablespoon sunflower oil

Using kitchen paper, blot a small crêpe pan with oil. Place over a medium-high heat while you prepare the batter.

Put the flour, almond milk, sugar, salt, and oil into a bowl and whisk until combined and foamy.

Add 2 tablespoons of the light batter into the pan and carefully tip the pan from side to side, then up and down to evenly distribute the batter. Cook for about 1 minute until lightly golden, then carefully flip the crêpe and cook for a further minute. Add small amounts of extra oil to the pan as required and repeat this step until all the mixture has been used.

lime and coconut syllabub

serves 2 generously

This simple, five-ingredient syllabub is rich and creamy with a hint of zesty lime. Serve chilled in glasses for the perfect minimalist dessert.

Chilling a can of coconut milk will separate the cream from the water, so you can simply scoop out the cream to make the most delicious desserts.

400ml (14fl oz) can full-fat coconut milk, chilled

4 tablespoons coconut yoghurt

2 tablespoons maple syrup

2 unwaxed limes

1 teaspoon toasted coconut chips

Open the can of chilled coconut milk and scoop out the solid cream, discarding the remaining coconut water (or reserve it for another recipe). Spoon the coconut cream into a mixing bowl and add the coconut yoghurt. Use an electric whisk to whip the cream, yoghurt, and maple syrup together for about 5 minutes until gentle peaks begin to form.

In the meantime, finely grate the lime zest, then halve one of the limes, ready for juicing.

Stir the lime zest through the creamy mixture (reserving a teaspoon for serving), then squeeze in the juice of ½ lime.

Spoon into dessert glasses and top with a few toasted coconut chips and lime zest to serve.

blackberry mojito

serves 1

Something tall, dark, and handsome – for one!

Using ripe blackberries will allow the tart flavour of the fruit to come through, with minimal effort and maximum enjoyment.

In a tall glass, add the blackberries, sugar, and mint leaves. Chop the lime in half and squeeze in the juice through a sieve, muddling together the ingredients with a stirrer or spoon.

Pour in the rum and ice, followed by the soda water. Enjoy immediately.

6 ripe blackberries

1 tablespoon caster (superfine) sugar

6 fresh mint leaves

1 unwaxed lime

50ml (2fl oz/¼ cup) white rum

2 tablespoons crushed ice

200ml (7fl oz/scant 1 cup) chilled sparkling soda water

summer punch slushie

serves 2

What a way to bring back childhood memories of a playful summer, refreshed by a fruity icy drink. Everyone will love this fruity, chilled treat. Serve with a long spoon and a straw.

Pour the lemonade between two large dessert glasses.

Add two scoops of sorbet to each glass, followed by a slice of cucumber and orange.

Garnish with the mint leaves and serve immediately.

400ml (14fl oz/1¾ cups) chilled cloudy lemonade

4 scoops of raspberry sorbet

2 slices of cucumber

2 slices of unwaxed orange

4 fresh mint leaves

spiced rum and cinnamon grilled pineapple with coconut cream

serves 4

This simple pineapple is the perfect balance of sweet and spicy. Use a dark, spiced rum as it works brilliantly in conjunction with the woody cinnamon and brown caramelized sugar. This is a great addition to any barbecue.

Ripe pineapple is easy to prepare. Simply slice off the green top with a large knife. Then stand the pineapple on a flat surface and slice away the skin, following the contour of the fruit. Slice fingers of pineapple and discard the tough core.

100ml (3½fl oz/scant ½ cup) dark spiced rum

1 medium pineapple

2 teaspoons light brown sugar

1 teaspoon ground cinnamon

400ml (14fl oz) can full-fat coconut milk, chilled

Place a griddle pan over a medium heat.

Pour the rum into a wide bowl and set aside. Peel and chop the pineapple into fingers, then dip each slice into the rum to coat. Sprinkle with the brown sugar and cinnamon.

Using tongs, place the pineapple fingers onto the griddle pan and cook for 4–5 minutes on each side, allowing each side to caramelize.

While the pineapple is grilling, scoop out the thick coconut cream from the top of the can, discarding the remaining coconut water (or save it for another recipe). Scoop the coconut cream into a bowl, then beat it until thick and peaked using an electric whisk.

Serve immediately while the pineapple is hot and spoon over the coconut cream.

the lazy millionaire's shortbread pudding

serves 6

Millionaire's shortbread is a baked classic. This quick recipe was created when I planned to bake a batch for guests, but ran out of time. So I pressed the shortbread base into individual ramekins and served it at the table with hot caramel sauce and melted chocolate, for my guests to create themselves. It was a huge success! I know you are going to love it too.

Preheat the oven to 190°C/375°F/Gas 5.

Start by making the biscuit base. Combine the flour, sugar, and sea salt in a food processor, then add the vegan butter and mix until a dough is formed. Press the dough into 6 ramekins, in a 2cm (¾in) layer. Bake for 9–10 minutes until pale golden.

While the bases are cooking, make the caramel sauce. Put the sugar, golden syrup, vegan butter, and vanilla extract in a pan. Simmer over a medium heat for 4–5 minutes without stirring. Remove from the heat and allow to cool for 1 minute, then whisk in the soya cream. Pour into a jug and keep warm.

For the chocolate sauce, break up the chocolate into a heatproof bowl and blast in the microwave for 20 seconds, stir, then blast for 20 seconds more, or until fully melted. Whisk in the soya cream, then transfer into another jug and keep warm.

Remove the ramekins from the oven and serve immediately for a softer, cakier base, or allow to cool for a few minutes for a firmer base. Serve with the caramel and chocolate sauces and pour both into the ramekins just before enjoying while hot.

For the shortbread biscuit base
50g (1¾oz/scant ½ cup) plain (all-purpose) flour

1 tablespoon caster (superfine) sugar

pinch of fine sea salt

30g (1oz) vegan butter

For the caramel sauce
3 tablespoons soft brown sugar

2 tablespoons golden syrup

1 rounded tablespoon vegan butter

1 teaspoon vanilla extract

150ml (5fl oz/¾ cup) soya cream

For the chocolate sauce
200g (7oz) good-quality very dark chocolate

100ml (3½fl oz/scant ½ cup) soya cream

syrup sponge pudding

serves 2

Syrup sponge pudding has been a firm favourite of mine since childhood. I love the hot, sweet, and sticky syrup that soaks into the fluffy cake. My mum always made it in the microwave – and so do I.

Combining soya milk with cider vinegar creates a quick vegan buttermilk, perfect for a light, dairy-free cake.

100ml (3½fl oz/scant ½ cup) soya milk

1 teaspoon apple cider vinegar

50g (1¾oz/scant ¼ cup) caster (superfine) sugar

50g (1¾oz) vegan butter

100g (3½oz/¾ cup) self-raising (self-rising) flour

½ teaspoon baking powder

1 teaspoon vanilla extract

4 tablespoons golden syrup

Measure the soya milk into a jug and whisk in the vinegar. Set aside and allow it to curdle.

In a large bowl, cream together the sugar and vegan butter until pale and combined. Then add the flour and baking powder and bring together to a stiff mixture.

Spoon the vanilla extract into the curdled milk, then pour into the bowl. Stir to incorporate fully.

In a microwave-safe bowl, spoon in the golden syrup to form a layer at the bottom, then gently pour over the cake batter. Cook in a 800W microwave for 3 minutes until the sponge appears just set.

Allow to stand for 1 minute before carefully turning out onto a plate. Serve immediately.

st clement's mince pies

makes about 10

It's no great secret that I enjoy a mince pie or two. I tend to start my Christmas feasting in early November, baking up batches of these fast mince pies for anyone visiting, to get them in the festive spirit. Jazz up a jar of sweet mincemeat with candied lemon peel and some orange zest. Most mincemeat is made with vegetable suet, but do check the ingredients before you buy.

1 sheet of ready-rolled puff pastry (ensure dairy free)

400g (14oz) jar good-quality sweet mincemeat (ensure vegetable suet)

1 rounded tablespoon candied lemon peel

2 teaspoons orange liqueur

zest of 1 unwaxed orange, grated

1 tablespoon soya milk

icing (confectioners') sugar, to dust

Preheat the oven to 220°C/425°F/Gas 7.

Lay the puff pastry sheet on a flat surface and use a round 5cm (2-in) cutter to press out pastry disks. Place them directly onto a baking tray. Using a smaller 4cm (1½in) cutter, press gently into the centre of each pastry disk to leave a light indentation – this shouldn't cut through the pastry.

Spoon the mincemeat into a bowl and mix in the candied lemon peel and orange liqueur. Stir through the orange zest.

Spoon a small amount of the mincemeat into the centre of the pastry disks, then brush a little soya milk over the pastry edges.

Bake for 10–11 minutes until golden and the pastry has puffed up around the sides. Dust with icing sugar before serving.

2 minute chocolate chip and pecan cookie

serves 1

Yes, you read that correctly! You will have this comforting cookie in just 2 minutes. Like any cookie, it will harden as it cools, however, if you want a warm, soft-centre cookie eat it immediately. Or feel free to wait 5 minutes until the edges crisp a little. I think it's incredible served with a scoop of non-dairy vanilla ice cream.

Many supermarkets sell dark chocolate chips that are accidentally vegan. If you don't have any to hand, chop up two squares of a dark chocolate bar to use in place of the chocolate chips.

1 rounded tablespoon vegan butter

2 tablespoons soft brown sugar

1 teaspoon vanilla extract

1 tablespoon pecan nuts

4 tablespoons plain (all-purpose) flour

1 tablespoon dark chocolate chips

In a microwave-safe bowl, spoon in the vegan butter and melt in an 850W microwave for 30 seconds.

Stir in the brown sugar, vanilla extract, pecan nuts, and plain flour into the melted vegan butter to form a dough, then stir through the chocolate chips.

Spoon the mixture as a single cookie onto a microwave-safe plate, then microwave for 1 minute 30 seconds until cooked.

chai tea poached pears

serves 4

This recipe came about by accident when I bought a bag full of pears from my local market, went home to poach them, and realized I had no red wine. To match the tannin taste of red wine, I substituted the alcohol for black tea and all the spices I had in the cupboard. The pears soak up the sweet, hearty spices and are a perfect last-minute dessert that looks and tastes impressive.

Pour the black tea into a large pan and add the sugar, star anise, cardamom pods, cinnamon sticks, cloves, nutmeg, mixed spice, and vanilla paste. Bring to the boil over a high heat.

In the meantime, cut the base of the pears so that they can sit flat and peel away the skin. Use tongs to gently place each pair into the pan.

Reduce the heat slightly and allow to cook for 10–12 minutes until the pears are soft. Serve immediately with a generous spoonful of the fragrant syrup from the pan.

1 litre (1¾ pints/4 cups) black tea

3 tablespoons caster (superfine) sugar

4 star anise

6 cardamom pods

2 cinnamon sticks

2 cloves

1 teaspoon grated nutmeg

1 teaspoon ground mixed spice

1 teaspoon vanilla paste

4 ripe Conference pears

cheat's strawberry balsamic jam

makes 1 small jar

When you don't have the time to make a special homemade jam – cheat. Adding a couple of extra ingredients to shop-bought strawberry jam will transform it (and no one will know you didn't spend hours stirring a hot pan). A touch of balsamic vinegar enhances the flavour of sweet strawberries and lends a lovely rich colour to the jam. Serve generously on Traditional sultana scones (see page 112).

200g (7oz/1½ cups) fresh strawberries, hulled and halved

5 tablespoons strawberry jam

1 tablespoon balsamic vinegar

Put all the ingredients into a large saucepan and cook over a low-medium heat for 10 minutes, stirring occasionally until the fresh strawberries have cooked down and the ingredients have combined.

Serve warm or allow to cool before storing in a sterilized airtight jar for up to two weeks.

essentials

guacamole
tomato, red onion, and coriander salsa
chilli salt tortilla chips
smoky tomato pan-chutney
beetroot ketchup
red cabbage and apple slaw
paprika-roasted crispy kale
roasted tomato and rosemary sauce
olive tapenade
lemon and almond pesto
sumac onion salad
edamame fried rice
coconut and lemongrass rice
cauliflower and dill mash
caramelized red onion houmous
tenderstem broccoli with orange and chilli
pomegranate, cucumber, and mint relish
lime and chive salad dressing
red wine reduction
cranberry and orange sauce

guacamole

serves 2 generously

Guacamole should be chunky, rustic, and full of flavour. Mash the ingredients with a fork and get your hands involved to combine this traditional Mexican side dish.

There's no need to peel and chop the avocado, simply use a spoon to scoop out the ripe flesh.

Put the tomato and onion into a bowl.

Finely chop half the chilli and reserve the rest for another recipe. Add the chopped chilli to the bowl.

Halve the avocados and spoon out the flesh into the bowl, then mash the ingredients together.

Mix the coriander into the guacamole. Slice the lime in half and squeeze the juice through a sieve into the bowl before stirring through. Season with salt.

1 large tomato, finely chopped

1 small red onion, finely chopped

½ small red chilli, halved and deseeded

2 ripe avocados

generous handful of fresh coriander (cilantro), roughly chopped

1 unwaxed lime

generous pinch of sea salt flakes

tomato, red onion, and coriander salsa

serves 4

Fresh, homemade salsa is not only delicious but simple to prepare. Serve as a dip or load inside a sandwich for a fiery filling.

300g (10oz) ripe tomatoes, chopped

1 red onion, finely chopped

1 red chilli, halved, deseeded and finely sliced

handful of fresh coriander (cilantro), torn

1 unwaxed lime

pinch of sea salt

Place the tomatoes, onion, chilli, and coriander in a bowl.

Cut the lime in half, then squeeze in the juice through a sieve. Sprinkle over the salt and stir to combine all the ingredients.

chilli salt tortilla chips

serves 2 generously

These crispy chips are the perfect weekend snack and a great way to use up tortillas.

2 soft tortillas

2 tablespoons olive oil

½ teaspoon dried chilli flakes

½ teaspoon smoked salt flakes

Preheat the oven to 180°C/350°F/Gas 4.

Slice the tortillas into triangles and arrange in a single layer on a baking tray, or two if needed.

Drizzle over the oil and gently rub onto the triangles.

Sprinkle over the chilli flakes and smoked salt, then bake for 5–6 minutes until the edges are golden and crisp.

smoky tomato pan-chutney

serves 2

Some dishes just call out for a tangy side of tomato chutney and my version cooks in just 10 minutes. I love serving it warm.

Worcestershire sauce adds a splash of spices in an instant. Although, some Worestershire sauce brands contain anchovies, so be sure that you use a sauce that is suitable for vegans.

Add the tomatoes to a pan, along with their seeds and juice, and 5 tablespoons cold water.

Add the Worcestershire sauce, sugar, smoked paprika, and hot chilli sauce.

Cook over a medium-high heat for 10 minutes, breaking up the tomato chunks as you stir.

8 ripe red tomatoes, finely chopped

2 teaspoons vegan Worcestershire sauce

½ teaspoon caster (superfine) sugar

½ teaspoon smoked paprika

2–3 drops of hot chilli sauce

beetroot ketchup

serves 4 generously

This vivid pink beetroot ketchup is a flavour twist on a classic ketchup, which is wonderful served with my Vegetable box pie with butter bean mash (see page 86).

Add the beetroot to a pan along with any excess beetroot juice.

Stir in the vinegar, thyme, and nutmeg and cook for 10 minutes over a medium heat.

Remove from the heat and tip the mixture into a blender. Pour in the oil and whizz until smooth and puréed.

300g (10oz) cooked beetroot, roughly chopped

1 tablespoon malt vinegar

½ teaspoon dried thyme

¼ teaspoon nutmeg

2 tablespoons extra virgin olive oil

red cabbage and apple slaw

serves 4

This slaw has the right balance of sweet and sharp, making it the perfect accompaniment to just about anything.

You'll find apple cider vinegar near the oils and dressings in most major supermarkets and high-street health-food shops.

300g (10oz) red cabbage, coarsely shredded

2 Granny Smith apples, grated

3 spring onions (scallions), finely chopped

1 tablespoon apple juice

2 teaspoons apple cider vinegar

1 teaspoon Dijon mustard

Place the cabbage in a large bowl.

Combine the apples and spring onions with the cabbage.

Spoon in the apple juice, apple cider vinegar, and mustard, then stir through to combine.

paprika-roasted crispy kale

serves 2 generously

I love this crispy kale served with Pad Thai jay with lime and sesame (see page 106), although it makes a pretty good snack on its own too.

Buy a bag of pre-shredded kale to roast, to save time chopping the larger kale leaves.

1 tablespoon olive oil

½ teaspoon paprika

pinch of sea salt flakes

200g (7oz) kale, shredded

Preheat the oven to 180°C/350°F/Gas 4.

Mix the oil, paprika, and salt in a bowl. Add in the kale and gently coat in the oil mix.

Place the kale onto a baking sheet in a single layer without overlapping so it cooks evenly. Bake for 7 minutes, then remove the tray and shake to distribute the oil, then bake for another 2 minutes until crisp.

roasted tomato and rosemary sauce

serves 2

Sweet plum tomatoes and woody rosemary are a beautiful flavour marriage. Use this sauce to stir through pasta, add to a pizza, or drizzle over Mediterranean vegetables.

Preheat the oven to 200°C/400°F/Gas 6.

Arrange the whole tomatoes on a baking tray. Add the onion and whole garlic clove to the tray and sprinkle with the rosemary. Drizzle with olive oil, then roast for 12–13 minutes until the tomatoes have softened.

Spoon the tomatoes, onion, and garlic into a blender. Pour in the extra virgin olive oil and blend on a high setting until smooth and creamy. Season with salt and black pepper.

300g (10oz) baby plum tomatoes

1 onion, roughly chopped

1 clove of garlic, peeled

½ teaspoon dried rosemary

drizzle of olive oil, for roasting

50ml (2fl oz/¼ cup) good-quality extra virgin olive oil

pinch of sea salt and black pepper

olive tapenade

serves 2

Whether it's an accompaniment to a sliced baguette and a glass of wine, or part of a tapas dinner, this tapenade will have everyone dreaming of summer.

Add the olives and capers to a food processor.

Cut the lemon in half and squeeze in the juice through a sieve.

Pour in the oil and blitz until semi-smooth.

200g (7oz/2 cups) stoned (pitted) mixed olives

1 tablespoon capers, rinsed

1 unwaxed lemon

4 tablespoons good-quality extra virgin olive oil

lemon and almond pesto

serves 2

I always have a jar of this moreish pesto in the refrigerator as it's so delicious and versatile. Stir it through pasta, spoon over bruschetta, or use as a dip for breadsticks.

Put the garlic and basil into a blender or food processor with the flaked almonds.

Grate the zest of the lemon into the mix, then halve the lemon and squeeze in the juice through a sieve.

Pour in the oil, then blitz until almost smooth. Season with salt.

1 clove of garlic, peeled

30g (1oz) fresh basil leaves, torn

50g (1¾oz/generous ½ cup) flaked (slivered) almonds

1 unwaxed lemon

150ml (5fl oz/⅔ cup) good-quality extra virgin olive oil

pinch of sea salt

sumac onion salad

serves 4

Sumac is a ground blend of bright sumac berries, grown in warmer climates. It has a fresh, lemony flavour and is a traditional ingredient in Middle-Eastern cuisine. I think it tastes more like lemon than lemon itself! Serve with falafel, houmous, and flatbreads.

Finely slice both the onions. Add to a bowl and sprinkle with the sumac.

Stir the parsley and mint through the onions.

Halve the lemon and squeeze in the juice through a sieve. Pour in the olive oil and stir to combine.

Allow the salad to infuse for 10 minutes, then season with salt.

1 red onion

1 white onion

1 teaspoon ground sumac

generous handful of fresh flat-leaf parsley, finely chopped

4–5 fresh mint leaves, finely chopped

1 unwaxed lemon

1 tablespoon extra virgin olive oil

pinch of sea salt

edamame fried rice

serves 2

This fresh and colourful rice makes an excellent side dish to my Sweet and sour with cashews (see page 88). You won't miss the egg fried into the mix as the mushrooms provide an awesome earthy flavour and soft texture.

140g (5oz/¾ cup) basmati rice

6 chestnut (cremini) mushrooms

4 spring onions (scallions)

1 carrot

3 tablespoons fresh or frozen edamame beans

1 tablespoon sunflower oil

2 tablespoons light soy sauce

Add the rice to a saucepan and cover with hot water. Boil for 10 minutes over a medium-high heat until fluffy.

In the meantime, finely chop the mushrooms and spring onions. Grate the carrot coarsely and set aside. If using frozen edamame beans, defrost them; if using fresh, ensure the shells are removed.

Heat the oil in a wok over a high heat. Add the mushrooms, spring onions, carrot, and edamame beans and stir-fry for 2 minutes.

When the rice is cooked, remove it from the heat and drain thoroughly. Carefully toss the rice into the wok and combine with the vegetables.

Spoon in the soy sauce and stir-fry for a further minute. Serve immediately.

coconut and lemongrass rice

serves 2

Delicate Thai flavours of lemongrass and coconut infuse fragrant basmati rice for an effortless side dish.

1 stalk of lemongrass

150g (5½oz/¾ cup) basmati rice

400ml (14fl oz) can full-fat coconut milk

1 tablespoon desiccated (shredded) coconut

Gently bruise the lemongrass until fragrant using the back of a spoon.

Add the lemongrass stalk, rice, coconut milk, and 100ml (3½fl oz/scant ½ cup) water to a pan, then bring to the boil over a high heat. When boiling, reduce to a simmer and cover with a lid. Cook for 10–12 minutes until the liquid has been absorbed, stirring occasionally to prevent sticking.

Remove and discard the lemongrass stalk. Stir through the coconut and serve immediately.

cauliflower and dill mash

serves 2

When you're in a hurry, mashed potato is out of the question. However, if you simply swap potato for cauliflower, and blitz it with some creamy ingredients, you can soon enjoy that comforting taste in under 15 minutes. You will find non-dairy cream cheese in many large supermarkets, with many stocking more than one brand.

If you don't have time to get mashing, simply pop all the ingredients into a food processor and blitz until smooth.

Bring a pan of water to the boil while you remove the stem of the cauliflower. Add the florets to the water and boil for 10 minutes until completely softened.

Thoroughly drain the water and add the dill and cream cheese to the pan. Mash the cauliflower until smooth and creamy, then season with salt and black pepper.

1 cauliflower

½ tablespoon fresh dill, finely chopped

3 tablespoons non-dairy cream cheese

pinch of sea salt and black pepper

caramelized red onion houmous

serves 2 generously

Once you try this, you'll never choose shop-bought houmous again. Invest in a good-quality tahini, which is creamy rather than set. Chickpeas that are jarred rather than canned are easier to whip into houmous, and they also provide a smoother texture. Serve with warmed pitta breads.

This houmous will keep in the refrigerator for up to three days.

1 tablespoon olive oil

1 red onion, finely sliced

600g (1¼lb) canned chickpeas (garbanzo beans), rinsed and drained

2 cloves of garlic, crushed

3 tablespoons good-quality tahini

1 unwaxed lemon

pinch of ground cumin

pinch of za'atar

generous drizzle of extra virgin olive oil

Heat the olive oil in a pan over a low-medium heat. Add the onion to the pan and slowly cook down for 8 minutes.

Tip the chickpeas into a bowl. Cover with boiling water and allow to sit while the onion is cooking. This process will make a smoother houmous.

Add the garlic to the pan and cook for a further 2 minutes, until the onion is starting to brown.

Tip half the onion and garlic mixture into a blender, along with the tahini. Drain the hot water from the chickpeas and add to the blender. Chop the lemon in half and squeeze in the juice through a sieve. Blend until smooth.

Stir through the remaining onion and garlic mixture along with the cumin and za'atar. Drizzle over the extra virgin olive oil just before serving.

tenderstem broccoli with orange and chilli

serves 2

Purple sprouting broccoli and sugar snap peas are stir-fried with freshly squeezed orange juice, hot chilli, and crushed nuts in this side dish that packs a flavour punch. You'll find pre-chopped nuts in health-food shops and some supermarkets, or make your own by whizzing a handful of mixed nuts in a food processor.

As a side dish, this recipe serves two people. Serve it up for one with some noodles for a quick yet substantial lunch.

1 tablespoon sunflower oil

8 stems of tenderstem broccoli, stalk ends trimmed

handful of sugar snap peas

1 teaspoon dried chilli flakes

1 unwaxed orange

1 tablespoon mixed chopped nuts

handful of fresh coriander (cilantro), roughly chopped

Heat the oil in a wok until hot.

Throw the broccoli into the hot wok along with the sugar snap peas and chilli flakes, and stir-fry on high for 5 minutes.

Slice the orange in half and squeeze over half the juice through a sieve, reserving the other half of the orange for another recipe. Add the nuts and stir through for 1 minute.

Remove from the heat and scatter with the coriander just before serving.

pomegranate, cucumber, and mint relish

serves 2 generously

Refreshing and cooling, this simple relish is best served with my Chickpea, apricot and maple-pan tagine (see page 100).

To make pomegranate seed removal easy, massage the skin of the fruit before slicing it in half, then firmly tapping it into a bowl.

Slice the pomegranate in half and tap out the juicy seeds.

Chop the cucumber into small chunks. Add it to the pomegranate along with the mint and stir to combine.

1 pomegranate

10cm (4in) piece of cucumber

5–6 fresh mint leaves, finely chopped

lime and chive salad dressing

serves 2

This zesty salad dressing is so simple to make and it works well with various salads, especially those with an eastern twist.

Spoon the oil into a lidded jar.

Finely grate the zest of the lime into the jar, then halve the lime and squeeze in the juice through a sieve.

Add the chives to the jar. Secure the lid and shake until combined. Season with black pepper.

6 tablespoons good-quality extra virgin olive oil

1 unwaxed lime

handful of chives, finely chopped

pinch of black pepper

red wine reduction

serves 2 generously

There are few things in life as luxurious as a red wine reduction. Rich, deep, and smooth, this elegant sauce is best served with a Sunday lunch, or with mashed potatoes and vegan sausages.

Add the pear and garlic to a large saucepan along with the wine, sugar, bay leaf, thyme, rosemary, and peppercorns.

Bring to the boil over a high heat, then reduce to a low simmer. Cook for 12–13 minutes until the wine has reduced down by more than half.

Strain through a sieve into a serving jug, discarding the other ingredients.

1 pear, roughly chopped

2 cloves of garlic, crushed

375ml (13fl oz/1⅔ cups) vegan red wine

1 tablespoon demerara sugar

1 bay leaf

1 teaspoon dried thyme

1 teaspoon dried rosemary

1 teaspoon whole black peppercorns

cranberry and orange sauce

serves 4

Not exclusive to Christmas, cranberry sauce is a simple fruit sauce that can be served with many dishes. I've even been known to load it onto veggie burgers! This is a family recipe that has been around for many years.

Coarsely zest the orange, then slice it in half and squeeze the juice into a pan through a sieve. Add the zest.

Tip in the cranberries and caster sugar and cook over a medium–high heat for 5 minutes, stirring frequently.

The sauce will thicken as it cools, so don't cook it for more than 5 minutes.

1 unwaxed orange

250g (9oz/2¾ cups) fresh or frozen cranberries

3 tablespoons caster (superfine) sugar

index

acknowledgements

Where do I start thanking everyone who has put this book together?

Firstly, a huge thank you to my publishing director Sarah Lavelle and editor Romilly Morgan for seeing my vision for this book – I've loved working with you. Thank you to creative director Helen Lewis for bringing the ideas to life and Nathan Grace and Nicola Ellis getting the pages spot on! Thank you to marketing manager Laura Willis and the publicity team for your ongoing work. A heartfelt thanks to everyone at Quadrille; you're talented, creative and a dream to work with.

Thank you to the incredible Dan Jones and his assistant Sophie Fox for the beautiful photography, what a privilege it was to work with you. Heartfelt thank you goes to Emily Ezekiel for the amazing food and prop styling and for being so fantastic to work with. Huge thanks to Becks Wilkinson and Anna Barnett for your expertise in the kitchen (even during the hottest week of 2016).

Thank you to my agent, Victoria Hobbs at A.M. Heath, for showing kindness and belief, as well as a fantastic sense of humour throughout the whole project.

To my incredible Mum and Dad, thank you for believing in me from the start. Without your support, I wouldn't have the confidence to believe in my dreams. Thank you also for letting me take over your kitchen on a regular basis and for the honest reviews of my kitchen triumphs and fails!

Thank you to my amazing sister Carolyne and wonderful brother-in-law Mark, who have shown generosity and love from day one. To my beautiful, cheeky twin nieces Tamzin and Tara, whom I love with all my heart – follow your dreams. Thank you to Auntie May for your words of encouragement.

Big love to my wonderful best friends Charlotte, Mary-Anne, Amelia and Louise. I'm so proud of your achievements, you are incredibly strong women. Thank you for your ever supportive (and amusing) friendships, cups of tea and text messages. To the best writing partner and housemate, Dudley the rabbit! Thanks for keeping me company and for all the cuddles.

Last but not least, David. I can never say thank you enough for believing in me, for all the practical help you give and for being happy to eat anything I cook, at any hour of the day or night. I love you and can't wait for our next chapter together.

publishing director: Sarah Lavelle
creative director: Helen Lewis
junior commissioning editor: Romilly Morgan
designers: Nathan Grace and Nicola Ellis
photographer: Dan Jones
food and props stylist: Emily Ezekiel
food stylist's assistant: Anna Barnett
production: Tom Moore, Vincent Smith

First published in 2017 by Quadrille, an imprint of Hardie Grant Publishing

Quadrille
52–54 Southwark Street
London SE1 1UN
quadrille.com

Reprinted in 2017 (six times), 2018 (seven times), 2019
18 17 16 15

Cataloguing in Publication Data: a catalogue record for this book is available from the British Library.

ISBN: 978 1 84949 963 7

Printed in Spain